Deali[...] EVIL P[...]WERS of your FATHER'S HOUSE

Dr. D. K. Olukoya

DR. D. K. OLUKOYA

Dealing With The Evil Powers Of Your Father's House

1st Printing - March, 2002 AD
DR. D. K. OLUKOYA
ISBN 978-35904-6-4

Published by:
The Battle Cry Christian Ministries

322, Herbert Macaulay Way,
Yaba P. O. Box 12272, Ikeja, Lagos.
Website: www.battlecryng.com
email: sales@battlecryng.com
Phone: 2348033044239

I salute my wonderful wife, Pastor Shade, for her invaluable support in the ministry.

I appreciate her unquantifiable support in the book ministry as the cover designer, art editor and art advisor
All Scripture quotation is from the King James Version of the Bible

Publications by Dr. D. K. Olukoya, published and marketed by The Battle Cry Christian Ministries

1. "Adura Agbayori" (Yoruba Version of the Second Edition of Pray Your Way to Breakthroughs).
2. "Awon Adura Ti Nsi Oke Didi" (Yoruba Prayer Book)
3. Be Prepared.
4. Breakthrough Prayers For Business Professionals.
5. Brokenness.
6. Comment Se Delivrer Soi-Meme (French Edition of How To Receive Personal Deliverance).
7. Criminals In The House of God.
8. Dealing With Local Satanic Technology.
9. Dealing With Witchcraft Barbers.
10. Dealing With Hidden Curses.
11. Dealing With The Powers of Your Father's House
12. Dealing With Unprofitable Roots.
13. Deliverance By Fire
14. Deliverance From Spirit Husband And Spirit Wife.
15. Deliverance of The Conscience
16. Deliverance of The Head.
17. Drawers of Power From The Heavenlies.
18. Evil Appetite
19. Fasting And Prayer.
20. Failure In The School Of Prayer.
21. For We Wrestle . . .
22. Holy Cry.
23. Holy Fever.
24. How To Obtain Personal Deliverance (Second Edition).
25. Let God Answer By Fire (Annual 70 Days Prayer and Fasting).
26. Limiting God.
27. Meat For Champions.
28. Overpowering Witchcraft.
29. Personal Spiritual Check-up.
30. POUVOIR CONTRE LES TERRORISTES SPIRITUELLES (French Edition of Power Against Spiritual Terrorists).

Publications by Dr. D. K. Olukoya, published and marketed by The Battle Cry Christian Ministries

31. Power Against Coffin Spirits.
32. Power Against Destiny Quenchers.
33. Power Against Dream Criminals
34. Power Against Local Wickedness.
35. Power Against Marine Spirits.
36. Power Against Spiritual Terrorists.
37. Power Must Change Hands.
38. Pray Your Way To Breakthroughs (Third Edition).
39. Prayer Rain.
40. Prayer Strategies For Spinsters And Bachelors.
41. Prayers To Destroy Diseases And Infirmities.
42. Prayers that Bring Explosive Increase (Annual 70 Days Prayer and Fasting).
43. Prayers To Mount Up With Wings As Eagles (Annual 70 Days Prayer and Fasting).
44. Prayers that Bring Miracles (Annual 70 Days Prayer and Fasting).
45. Prayers For Open Heaven, New Beginning and Fresh Fire (Annual 70 Days Prayer and Fasting).
46. PRIER JUSQU'A REMPORTER LA VICTOIRE (French Edition of Pray Your Way to Breakthroughs).
47. PRIERES DE PERCEE POUR LES HOMMES D'AFFAIRES (French Edition of Breakthroughs Prayers For Business Professionals).
48. Release From Destructive Covenants.
49. Revoking Evil Decrees.
50. Satanic Diversion Of The Black Race.
51. Smite The Enemy And He Will Flee.
52. Spiritual Warfare And The Home.
53. Strategic Praying.
54. Strategy Of Warfare Praying.
55. Students In The School Of Fear.
56. The Internal Stumbling Block.
57. The Lord Is A Man Of War.
58. The Prayer Eagle
59. The Slow Learners

Publications by Dr. D. K. Olukoya, published and marketed by The Battle Cry Christian Ministries

60. The Serpentine Enemies
61. The Vagabond Spirit.
62. The Great Deliverance.
63. The Spirit Of The Crab.
64. The Fire Of Revival.
65. The Tongue Trap.
66. Unprofitable Foundations.
67. Victory Over Satanic Dreams (Second Edition).
68. Violent Prayers Against Stubborn Situations.
69. When God Is Silent
70. Wealth Must Change Hands.
71. When You Are Knocked Down.
72. Your Foundation and Destiny

CONTENTS

Chapter 1

DEALING WITH THE EVIL POWERS OF YOUR FATHER'S HOUSE

1 Samuel 2:26-36:

And the child Samuel grew on, and was in favour both with the LORD, and also with men. 27And there came a man of God unto Eli, and said unto him, Thus saith the LORD, Did I plainly appear unto the house of thy father, when they were in Egypt in Pharaoh's house? 28And did I choose him out of all the tribes of Israel *to be* my priest, to offer upon mine altar, to burn incense, to wear an ephod before me? and did I give unto the house of thy father all the offerings made by fire of the children of Israel? 29Wherefore kick ye at my sacrifice and at mine offering, which I have commanded *in my* habitation; and honourest thy sons above me, to make yourselves fat with the chiefest of all the offerings of Israel my people? 30Wherefore the LORD God of Israel saith, I said indeed *that* thy house, and the house of thy father, should walk before me for ever: but now the LORD saith, Be it far from me; for them that honour me I will honour, and they that despise me shall be lightly esteemed. 31Behold, the days come, that I will cut off thine arm, and the arm of thy father's house, that there shall not be an old man in thine house. 32And thou shalt see an enemy *in my* habitation, in all *the wealth* which *God* shall give Israel: and there shall not be an old man in thine house for ever. 33And the man of thine, *whom* I shall not cut off from mine altar, *shall be* to consume thine eyes, and to grieve thine heart: and all the increase of thine house shall die in the flower of their age. 34And this *shall be* a sign unto thee, that shall come upon thy two sons, on Hophni and Phinehas; in one day they shall die both of them. 35And I will raise me up a faithful priest, *that* shall do according to *that* which *is* in mine heart and in my mind: and I will build him a sure house; and he shall walk before mine anointed for ever. 36And it shall come to pass, *that* every one that is left in thine house shall come *and* crouch to him for a piece of silver and a morsel of bread, and shall say, Put me, I pray thee, into one of the priests' offices, that I may eat a piece of bread.

Genesis 12:1-5:

Now the LORD had said unto Abram, Get thee out of thy country, and
from thy kindred, and from thy father's house, unto a land that I will
shew thee: [2]And I will make of thee a great nation, and I will bless thee,
and make thy name great; and thou shalt be a blessing: [3]And I will bless
them that bless thee, and curse him that curseth thee: and in thee shall
all families of the earth be blessed. [4]So Abram departed, as the LORD
had spoken unto him; and Lot went with him: and Abram *was* seventy and
five years old when he departed out of Haran. [5]And Abram took Sarai his
wife, and Lot his brother's son, and all their substance that they had
gathered, and the souls that they had gotten in Haran; and they went
forth to go into the land of Canaan; and into the land of Canaan they
came.

ANCESTRAL HOLD AND INFLUENCE

There is a very strong umbilical cord attaching every living being to his ancestors. Although you may have your own mind, you are a product of your ancestors. They have such a strong hold on you. Either you know it or not, the *powers of your father's house* have continued to exercise a very strong influence on your life and destiny. The average human being does not know enough of the history of his ancestors.

This explains why people suffer ignorantly.

The *power of your father's house* accounts for a greater percentage of the powers that are shaping and affecting your own destiny.

In the deliverance ministry, we have discovered that the lives of many people are ruled by wicked powers from the ancestral line. Many pastors have had their ministerial lives truncated at the prime of their ministry, simply because terrible power from their father's house decided to strike, by burying their ministerial calling.

A lot of people who are supposed to enjoy fantastic successes and breakthroughs have discovered that a lot of things are going upside down, simply because the power of their father's house is averse to their success.

Many women are suffering from problems related to marital turbulence. Whenever you discover certain strange things happening in your life, in spite of serious personal efforts, you must look beyond the physical and examine your foundation.

What may be happening to you may be things that are running through your family line, like a dark thread for some hundreds of years.

You may be a child of God, but if you have not dealt decisively with the evil influence from your father's house, you would be a candidate in the school of failure. This evil influence may stem from the legal ground created by your ancestors.

Our ancestors, have sold many of us into spiritual slavery. Once the deal has been sealed, you will continue to suffer even if you decide to change your geographical location.

Distance is No Barrier

In recent times, in my overseas ministration, I have listened to a lot of heart rendering stories. I have discovered that, many who believe that by going abroad they can escape evil attacks from home, only end up postponing the evil day. Distance is no barrier as far as evil powers are concerned.

The day you begin to deal with the *powers of your father's house* you will begin to experience the fulfilment of your destiny.

There is no denying the fact that many of our fore-fathers were wicked beyond comparison. Many of them served idols and made terrible covenants with very powerful spiritual entities. Again, a good number of them received terrible curses.

In many families powerful idols are still being worshipped till date. Since you cannot isolate yourself from your ancestors, their influence would affect you.

If you survey the entire gamut of travails in your life, you may observe that similar things are happening to your kindred.

Salient Points

The *powers of your father's house* may not prevent you from getting to the top. They may only strike and cause you to crash when you are about to attain the pinnacle of success.

Many people who would have been exceptional achievers are begging in order to eat. The powers of their father's house are applying remote control gadgets against them. The day God opens your eyes, to the wickedness of the *powers of your father's house*, you will begin to pray like you never did before.

The *power of your father's house* has no good plan whatsoever for you. No matter what happens they ensure that they programmed one negative thing or the other against every family member. They consult the family register and ensure that their evil programmes run through everyone who is linked by the same umbilical cord.

No Exception

No matter how educated you are, you are not excepted. Scientists, smart businessmen, those who are in the military, as well as those who have travelled all over the world, are all victims of the powers of their father's houses.

If you do not deal with these powers, you cannot really enjoy your life on earth. Even your Christian life will leave much to be desired. Something will keep on pulling you down even, when you are making serious efforts.

What many people need today is to take a leave of absence from everything and go for weeks of serious deliverance from the powers of their father's house.

Why is this necessary?

The *power of your father's house* might have been in existence for hundreds of years. Some of these spiritual entities have been carrying out their evil operation in the lives of many generations.

Even when people try to offer sacrifices to appease these evil powers, there is only respite for a while.

However, they will still strike again.

The *power of your father's house* is a very serious issue. Every effort spent to deal with it will yield great dividends.

Why Are We Addressing This Issue?

We are addressing this issue seriously because we know that there will be more international, continental, national, communal, family and personal breakthroughs and deliverance when we develop a new compendium of prayer points targeted at dealing with the powers of the father's house. Stubborn situations will receive divine touch, powerful entities will bow and millions of people will get off the grip of wicked powers, from their foundation.

Many prisoners will receive their freedom, buried destinies will be exhumed and turbulent cases will be divinely fixed up, as the powers of the father's house are kept under divine check.

This is one book that will cause ripples, in the kingdom of darkness.

THE *POWERS OF YOUR FATHER'S HOUSE*

What does the *power of your father's house* really mean? Is there any foundation Scripture, which will aid our understanding of this topic?

How can we really demystify the powerful entities, which we are considering in this chapter?

Let us go into the Scriptures.

It is good to pray, but your efforts may not yield any tangible result if you lack knowledge concerning the direction towards which you must send your prayer efforts.

Let me share a story with you in order to illustrate this point.

A sister went through serious travails in the area of marriage because she did not know how to pray against the power of her father's house. She couldn't get anyone to make marriage proposals to her until she was 37 years old. She became excited about the proposal. Strange enough, the man came later to say that he was no longer interested. That truncated her first effort towards getting married.

At age 39 she came across another fellow who was willing to get married to her. Just when they were planing to hold their wedding, a moving vehicle ran over him and he died instantly. For two years the lady battled with the trauma of her second attempt at getting married. At a point she vowed to remain single for life.

Somehow she decided to get married to another man at age 41. She found another man. They even succeeded in planning the wedding. Tragedy struck on the day of their wedding. The lady was dressed in immaculate wedding gown, while the man was dressed in a specially designed suit. The couple was beaming with smiles, not knowing what the powers of their father's house held in store for them.

The pastor stood up to read the marriage charge. He declared, "Is there is anybody here who have any reason or reasons why this couple should not be joined together in only matrimony? Let such a person speak out now or be silent forever."

There was silence. Then someone came forward saying: "I object. This marriage cannot take place. This man is my husband. This is our marriage certificate. Here are our children." The woman fainted. She never knew that the man who took her to the altar was married already.

The last experience made her to pray until she discovered the secret behind her inability to get married. She embarked on a serious prayer programme. One day, God gave her a revelation. She saw a woman in the labour room trying to deliver a baby. As soon as the woman was delivered of a baby girl someone came to congratulate her saying, "Congratulations! You have just had a beautiful baby girl."

The woman fumed saying: "Baby girl? I don't want to see it. Take that thing away."

The vision ended. Her mind flashed back to the story of her parents. Before her mother gave birth to her, she already had six girls. She was tired of having girls. By the time she got pregnant for the seventh time she wanted nothing but a male child. When her mother gave birth to her, she was referred to as a 'thing' and treated like an unwanted child. The power of her father's house trailed her until she discovered that something was wrong with her foundation. Meanwhile, she was busy making physical efforts when she was inside a spiritual cage.

This is exactly what is happening to many people today. I want you to close your eyes now and take this prayer point.

Every satanic transaction made on the day that I was born, die, in the name of Jesus.

Let me share a testimony with you, a lady had an unusual problem, which made her to pray with holy anger. Her problem was that at age 39, she has never seen her menstruation. Led by the spirit of God, I gave her one prayer point, 'every owner of evil load, carry your load, in the name of Jesus.'

God opened her eyes and she saw a revelation. She saw a woman carrying a load after being forced to do so by an angel. Her period started immediately. This lady battled with the strange problems until the evil load was removed from her.

Something happened in Abuja, Nigeria. A lady came to one of our special programmes and the Lord set her free from the powers of her father's house. The power of God moved as the Spirit of God. God led me to single her out, I simply stated: "The serpent troubling you has died. You are now free."

This woman lived in one of the high brow sections of the city. It is one of those places where we cannot find even the smallest snake. By the time she got home, she found a huge python lying dead on her bed. It was a strange sight. She later discovered that her forefathers were chronic snake worshippers. This is an example of the activities of the powers of the father's home.

The truth is that strange powers are residents in our father's home. Majority of those powers are negative. This negative powers have continued to constitute serious problems in the lives of many people.

Problems like failure, marital instability, demotion, destiny destruction, failure, career stagnation and the like are part of the problems issuing from the foundation of many people.

The power of your father's can make you to suffer from the cradle to the grave if you do not address these wicked powers.

They are also responsible for serious terrible condition.

PROBLEMS ASSOCIATED WITH THE EVIL *POWERS OF YOUR FATHER'S HOUSE*

Below are examples of problem emanating from the *power of your father's house.*

They are responsible for:

☞ Intense marital problems which many are going through today.

☞ Converting many into foot-mats that others use to climb up.

☞ The powers of seeing but not attaining.

☞ Making people live in cursed houses.

When you want to rent a house, they'll make sure you rent a room near an altar, or they'll make the person to build in a place where there is an altar.

The *powers of your father's house* can magnetise a person to demonic altars. Although the altar has been there for years.

☞ All the dreams of sitting for examinations and the

person never completes the examination.

☞ Financial embarrassment.

☞ Spiritual stagnation.

No matter how the person is trying to grow up or struggling to move he notices that these things are just not working.

☞ The burial of talents and virtues.

One of the tragedies of man is to see famous men suffering and begging for alms on the streets. Those who were once famous and talented now become destitutes.

☞ Non-cooperation's by would-be helpers.

You know that someone can help you but the fellow just refuses to help because the powers of your fathers house work against your receiving assistance. I pray that these powers would be broken today, in the name of Jesus.

☞ Constant business failure.

☞ Constant lack of working capital.

☞ Chain of problems.

As you are busy tackling one problem, another one is coming up.

☞ Desert prosperity.

You may look nice, well fed, comfortable, but you know that you just don't have anything.

☞ Conforming with evil family patterns.

☞ Being magnetised to debts.

Those who are indebted wake up in the morning before 4:00 o'clock and come back late at night in order to avoid being harassed.

☞ The dreams of retrogression.

☞ Evil diversions.

I have seen a lot of evil diversions. Some of the people who are supposed to be in their country and enjoying themselves, have travelled abroad and are suffering there. The enemy has removed them from the place of prosperity.

☞ Gradual dispossession.

So, if you discover that you have been selling off your

property, you better pray with holy madness. You are suffering from the *power of your father's house.*

☞ Poverty.

☞ Being cursed by a satanic prophet.

The powers of a person's house can manipulate a person to a place where they will put a curse on him. Many people go to the wrong church. If you tell them to leave, they can't leave because the powers of their father's house have put them in a cage. They give them church posts to tie them down. The enemy wants to destroy them.

☞ Strange and terrible infirmities.

I read about a lady in Europe. Their great-grandmother died of breast cancer, their grandmother died of breast cancer and her mother died of breast cancer. Because she didn't want to die of breast cancer. She now asked the doctors to remove her breast. They cut off the two breasts. Her thinking was that, if there is no breast for the cancer to attack, then nothing would have happened to her. The cancer attacked the liver. That is the power of her father's house.

☞ The vagabond spirit.

☞ Moving about with no hope at all.

☞ The mark of hatred in husbands or wives.

Your partner who used to love you so much before you married is now running after you with murderous intention.

☞ The problem of leaking pockets.

You may make money, but you don't know where it is going.

☞ All round attack of failures.

☞ Polluted children.

☞ Prayer paralysis.

☞ Spiritual blindness.

☞ Terrible dreams.

☞ Ministerial failures.

☞ Backsliding.

I want you to know that these are not things you can just

ignore. I've seen many strange things in my life. Most of these are from evil foundation. I have seen a woman with two sex organs. I have seen a 'menstruating man'. I have seen a 'speaking pregnancy'. None of them has shocked me beyond something that happened not too long ago.

A 70-year-old-preacher committed adultery with a girl of 20. This man has been serving the Lord for 50 years. Yet the enemy was able to pull him down. By the time this old man started his deliverance it was then he began to know where the problem was coming from; his father had 14 wives. The spirit of polygamy affected his background. The power of his father's house did not release him. Although he had been preaching for 50 years, he was not spared.

SCRIPTURAL EXAMPLES

Moses is an interesting figure. The Bible says in Genesis 49:5-7, that,

Simeon and Levi *are* brethren; instruments of cruelty *are in* their habitations. [6]O my soul, come not thou into their secret; unto their assembly, mine honour, be not thou united: for in their anger they slew a man, and in their selfwill they digged down a wall. [7]Cursed *be* their anger, for *it was* fierce; and their wrath, for it was cruel: I will divide them in Jacob, and scatter them in Israel.

Here you see Simeon and Levi. Two things were in their habitation. Cruelty and anger. In the cruelty and anger they became murderers, etc.

Let us read Exodus 2:1-2:

And there went a man of the house of Levi, and took *to wife* a daughter of Levi. [2]And the woman conceived, and bare a son: and when she saw him that he *was a* goodly *child*, she hid him three months.

The above verses will be read like this:

And there went a man from the house of cruelty and anger and took a wife a daughter of the house of cruelty and anger, so cruelty and anger plus cruelty and anger equals cruelty and anger. Who did they conceive? Moses and the problem of Moses started from there.

Moses led a fascinating and a distinguished life. Moses was the prince of Egypt. He was also the lawgiver. Moses was God's faithful servant, a man more humble than anyone else. Moses saw God face to face. He communicated God's word to the people. He was a spokesman, a Psalmist, and a prophet like no other. He was a child of a slave but lived in the palace like a king.

The man stammers when he talks to fellow men but when he is talking to God he speaks smoothly. He was a mighty warrior, he died alone on the mountain and then appeared again with Christ. No man assisted in the burial of Moses. It was God that buried him.

But in spite of all these, Moses ran into serious problems. Something was wrong with his foundation.

When Moses was in Egypt he took an Egyptian and killed him. You will wonder why. There was an evil flow from Levi, his father. Cruelty, anger and murder flew into his life. Moses killed an Egyptian just like his forefather Levi did.

Now, Moses went to the mountain and God gave him two tables of stones which God wrote by Himself. When Moses was coming down, he saw the people in a state he didn't like to see. He got so angry and smashed the two tablets of stone. The Bible says his anger waxed hot. He threw down on them stones that God wrote with His own fingers. We cannot see those tables again.

I don't know if God completely forgive Moses for what

he did. The flow continued. When Moses came down from the mountain he found the children of Israel worshipping down the golden calf. He got so annoyed, took the golden calf, grinded it into powder and put it in water. He forced the whole of Israel to drink that water.

His anger was strong enough to prevent him from entering the promised land. The powers in Moses father's house harassed his life at the edge of victory. Moses was a spiritual giant but the power of his father's house dealt with him.

It is interesting to note that, the fact that Moses had the privilege of being in the presence of God did not root out the evil powers of his father's house.

One can speak in tongues and prophesy, but these powers will still be there. Unless you take actions to pull them down and break them into pieces, they may ruin you.

Later satan came to contest for Moses' corpse. He said: "This is one of us; he has the spirit of anger. He's a murderer."

The powers of a person's father's house can cause so much confusion in his life, and prevent him from moving forward and attack him with the spirit of 'almost there'. It is a serious matter. If this could happen to Moses, we need to pray hard. I want you to know that the power in the father's house of Moses was what caused problems for him.

Abraham, told lies that his wife was not his wife. Isaac, his son told the same lies. Jacob told lies that he was Esau. The children of Jacob told lies that Joseph was dead. The sin of lying ran through their family line.

Judah had a very colourful destiny. There was a beautiful prophetic destiny concerning his tribe. He was to produce our Lord Jesus Christ. Judah was very important in the programme of God. The enemy discovered his wonderful destiny and worked very hard to hinder Judah.

I pray that, every power, working hard against your destiny shall be destroyed.

Judah got into foundational problems by marrying people that God told him not to marry. Satanic sexual perversion in the life of Judah was so pronounced that he committed fornication with his daughter-in-law. I mean Judah was going into prostitutes. This foundation destroyed many generations in the life of Judah.

We can now discover why David, who was supposed to go to the war front, decided to watch a satanic coloured television on the top of the roof. This demonic ancestral flow from his father's house led him to take another man's wife.

The thing went down to Solomon. Solomon had seven hundred wives and three hundred concubines. Although Solomon was a wise man, the powers of his father's house led him astray. These powers are very strong and powerful. Solomon had about one thousand women.

The same trend went down to Absalom the son of David. He was busy sleeping with his father's wife. It was an immoral flow. If these powers can deal with this man, we need to pray.

The satanic immoral flow in the life of Judah also pursued his children. Even at David's old age, he still required a young lady to keep him warm.

There would be no great ministry and manifestation of the power of God without great deliverance of our personal life. WE would not break away from the satanic flow of our parents and ancestors.

Judges 6:25:

And it came to pass the same night, that the LORD said unto him, Take thy father's young bullock, even the second bullock of seven years old, and throw down the altar of Baal that thy father hath, and cut down the grove that *is* by it:

God had called Gideon into the ministry of deliverance of God's people. He was a mighty man of valour. But he was completely under demotion organised by the idols of his father's house. First assignment God gave to Gideon was to destroy the idols of his father's house, which were negatively affecting his destiny.Unfortunately, many of us are still being controlled by the idols of our father's house. We need to break free by fire. Gideon could not move forward in his calling, until he carried out this important assignment.

2 Kings 5:27:

The leprosy therefore of Naaman shall cleave unto thee, and unto thy seed for ever. And he went out from his presence a leper *as white* as snow.

Here a curse was issued by Prophet Elisha upon Gehazi. Gehazi and his offsprings were to be eternal lepers. The evil power of Gehazi's house was the power of leprosy. If an offspring of Gehazi was to attend a healing service, the minister would not be able to help him, unless he reverses back to the curse issued by Elisha and deals with it.

Beloveth, it is time to arise, carry out a personal spiritual analysis, carry out spiritual mapping of your family life and deal with the evil powers therein.

SYMPTOMS OF STRANGULATIONS BY THE *EVIL POWERS OF YOUR FATHER'S HOUSE*

☞ When all inputs and efforts fail to get success.

☞ Instead of going forward, you are going backward.

☞ Unexplainable loss of memory.

☞ When men who should be winners fail.

☞ When you are governed by a power contrary to your will.

☞ A rich person suddenly turns poor.

☞ Continuous duping.

- ☞ When trials refuse to come to an end.
- ☞ Enslaving habits. E.g. sexual immorality.
- ☞ Unnatural movements in parts of the body.
- ☞ Inability to get baptised in the Holy Ghost.
- ☞ When problems are encountered in chain.
- ☞ Those who are demonised.
- ☞ Those who have horrible experiences in their dreams.
- ☞ Those who have participated in non-Christian religions.
- ☞ Sexual problems - confusion.
- ☞ Sick tongues.
- ☞ Emotional disturbances.
- ☞ Sicknesses defying medical diagnosis and treatment.
- ☞ Mental confusion.
- ☞ Restlessness.
- ☞ Hearing strange voices.

☞ Unholy fears.

☞ Failures.

☞ Operating under evil covenants and curses.

☞ Unexplainable family break down.

☞ Failure in Christian life.

☞ Profitless hardwork.

☞ Inherited problems.

☞ Constant harassment by evil spirits.

☞ Evil trend of problems in the family.

☞ Failure at the edge of success.

☞ Ungodly soul tie.

☞ After going through the normal channels of prayers, spiritual discipline, applying the word, etc., and victory is slow or non-existent.

SPIRITUAL HOSPITAL FOR TREATMENT

Organise your prayer strategies to cover the following items.

☞ Complete and deep repentance.

☞ Cancel any agreement made by your ancestors with demonic forces.

☞ Reject every spiritual marriage with dark spirits. E.g. water spirits.

☞ Terminate all satanic priesthood.

☞ Raise a new priesthood.

☞ Shake the foundations of all that is hidden in the heavenlies against you.

☞ Remove all covenants and agreements made by the people and their ancestors.

☞ Wipe out all satanic demands, covenants and agreements with your ancestors.

☞ Wipe out all evil programmes.

☞ Cut off all unbiblical blood covenants.

- ☞ Speak God's blessing over the land.
- ☞ Take the keys from the strongman.
- ☞ Close the gates against the strongman.
- ☞ Ask God to change the gatekeepers.
- ☞ Proclaim that creation will no longer respond to wicked voices.
- ☞ Dedicate the gates to God.
- ☞ Bind the spirits supervising the altars.
- ☞ Release the captives of this altar.
- ☞ Speak to the water spirits that cause disasters.
- ☞ Re-dedication.

PRAYER POINTS

1. I fire back, every arrow of my family idols, in the name of Jesus.
2. Every evil power, from my father's house, die, in the

name of Jesus.

3. Every evil power, from my mother's house, die, in the name of Jesus.
4. Let God arise, and let stubborn problems die, in the name of Jesus.
5. Every cycle of hardship, break, in the name of Jesus.
6. Where is the Lord God of Elijah, arise and manifest Your power, in the name of Jesus.
7. The voice of my enemy will not prevail over my destiny, in the name of Jesus.
8. Every terror of the night, scatter, in the name of Jesus.
9. Every witchcraft challenge of my destiny, die, in the name of Jesus.
10. Every seed of the enemy in my destiny, die, in the name of Jesus.
11. Every dream of demotion, die, in the name of Jesus.
12. Power of God, uproot wicked plantations from my life, in the name of Jesus.
13. Every destiny vulture, vomit my breakthroughs, in the name of Jesus.

14. Every evil power, that pursued my parents, release me, in the name of Jesus.
15. I fire back, every witchcraft arrow fired into my life as a baby, in the name of Jesus.
16. Fire of God, thunder of God, purse my pursuers, in the name of Jesus.
17. Holy Ghost fire, purge my blood from satanic injection, in the name of Jesus.
18. Every evil power of my father's house, that will not let me go, die, in the name of Jesus.
19. Every power designed to spoil my life, scatter, in the name of Jesus.
20. Every herbal power, working against my destiny, die, in the name of Jesus.
21. I kill, every sickness in my life, in the name of Jesus.
22. Every power, of the idols of my father's house, die, in the name of Jesus.
23. Every evil power, pursuing me from my father's house, die, in the name of Jesus.
24. Every evil power, pursuing me from my mother's house, die, in the name of Jesus.

25. Every witchcraft tree binding my placenta, die, in the name of Jesus.

26. Where is the Lord God of Elijah, arise and fight for me, in the name of Jesus.

27. Every destiny-demoting dreams, scatter, in the name of Jesus.

28. Every foundational bondage, break, in the name of Jesus.

29. Every dream sponsored by witchcraft, die, in the name of Jesus.

30. Every witchcraft vulture, vomit my destiny, in the name of Jesus.

31. Every problem, designed to destroy my destiny, die, in the name of Jesus.

32. Evil strangers, come of my destiny, in the name of Jesus.

33. In the presence of those asking fro my God, O God arise and manifest Your power, in the name of Jesus.

34. Every satanic animal programmed into my dream, die, in the name of Jesus.

35. Every herbalist searching for my face, receive the fire

of God, in the name of Jesus.

36. Every serpent and scorpion poison in my destiny, come out and die, in the name of Jesus.

37. Arise in my life, O God, and let the world know that You are my God, in the name of Jesus.

38. Every seed of witchcraft in my destiny, die, in the name of Jesus.

39. Every enemy of my increase and destiny, scatter, in the name of Jesus.

40. Every enemy of progress within me, scatter, in the name of Jesus.

Chapter 2

SLUMBERING IN THE TENT OF YOUR FATHER'S HOUSE

The title of this chapter may sound strange to you but you will realise what it is all about as you go on. Meanwhile I will quote some Scriptures, beginning with the book of Jeremiah 48:11:

Moab hath been at ease from his youth, and he hath settled on his lees, and hath not been emptied from vessel to vessel, neither hath he gone into captivity: therefore his taste remained in him, and his scent is not changed.

God has a message for everyone reading this book. There are also some specific persons for whom God has this message for. Moab had problems. He had always lived a life of ease, he had settled on his knees, he had not been emptied from vessel to vessel, he had never gone into captivity.

It is when a man has gone into captivity and has come out of it that he knows the value of freedom. Many people whose parents got born again before they were born would not understand what is called bondage. But when someone has been dipped into darkness and has been out of it, he automatically appreciates the value of freedom.

Moab had never been into captivity, so his taste remained unaltered; his flavour was not changed. The long and short of the matter is that Moab had been slumbering in the tent of his fathers. Moab had refused to change.

Unfortunately, there are many that are still slumbering in the tens of their fathers, and like a drunken man or a man under an evil spell, they are cleverly following the evil pattern that destroyed their fathers.

If you look at the book of Luke 7:31-34, Jesus too complained that there are people like this who are slumbering in the tents of their fathers:

Luke 7:31-34:

And the Lord said, Whereunto then shall I liken the men of this generation? and to what are they like? 32They are like unto children sitting in the marketplace, and calling one to another, and saying, We have piped unto you, and ye have not danced; we have mourned to you, and ye have not wept. 33For John the Baptist came neither eating bread nor drinking wine; and ye say, He hath a devil. 34The Son of man is come eating and drinking; and ye say, Behold a gluttonous man, and a winebibber, a friend of publicans and sinners!

The bottom line of what Jesus was saying is that this generation is slumbering in the tent of its father. There are many things happening around us now. We have piped unto people and they had refused to dance, we have mourned unto people, they have refused to weep. The bottom line is that there is no change, and this is very sad.

Le us look at more of the troubles of Moab as recorded in Isaiah 16:6:

We have heard of the pride of Moab; *he is* very proud: *even* of his haughtiness, and his pride, and his wrath: *but* his lies *shall* not *be* so."

Verse 12

And it shall come to pass, when it is seen that Moab is weary on the high place, that he shall come to his sanctuary to pray; but he shall not prevail.

Moab has refused to change; he was slumbering in the tent of his fathers. You may then ask the question: "What is the origin of Moab?".

In Genesis 19:29-38, we can see where the problems of Moab started from so that you too can know how to cry unto the Lord today.

And it came to pass, when God destroyed the cities of the plain, that
God remembered Abraham, and sent Lot out of the midst of the
overthrow, when he overthrew the cities in the which Lot dwelt. [30]And
Lot went up out of Zoar, and dwelt in the mountain, and his two
daughters with him; for he feared to dwell in Zoar: and he dwelt in a
cave, he and his two daughters. [31]And the firstborn said unto the
younger, Our father *is* old, and *there is* not a man in the earth to come
in unto us after the manner of all the earth: [32]Come, let us make our
father drink wine, and we will lie with him, that we may preserve seed of
our father. [33]And they made their father drink wine that night: and the
firstborn went in, and lay with her father; and he perceived not when she
lay down, nor when she arose. [34]And it came to pass on the morrow, that

the firstborn said unto the younger, Behold, I lay yesternight with my
father: let us make him drink wine this night also: and go thou in, *and* lie
with him, that we may preserve seed of our father. 35And they made
their father drink wine that night also: and the younger arose, and lay
with him; and he perceived not when she lay down, nor when she arose.
36Thus were both the daughters of Lot with child by their father. 37And
the firstborn bare a son, and called his name Moab: the same *is* the
father of the Moabites unto this day. 38And the younger, she also bare
a son, and called his name Benammi: the same *is* the father of the
children of Ammon unto this day.

Now we know the origin of Moab. The origin of Moab was in the city of Sodom and Gomorrah. It was someone trying to compromise his faith amongst Godless people.

Its origin was in a city filled with sexual immorality, sin, abomination and sodomy. The origin of Moab was when God asked a man to get out of a place and the man didn't want to get out and he lost his wife.

Its origin was in the fact that God asked a man to go out to the mountain but man preferred the valley. It was in drunkenness, incest, and deception with wine to commit atrocities.

So Moab had a lot of terrible things in his background. That would not have been a problem if Moab had decided to change.

There were people with more terrible backgrounds in the Bible. After all, the father of Hezekiah was the best king in the Bible, but Manasseh was a terrible wizard, a very occultic man. In fact, the Bible gave him a special place. But Hezekiah determined not to clumber in the tents of his father, and he jumped out of that evil tent, and so we read good things about him today.

We need to read the Bible very well. There are several cries in the Scriptures. Look at those men who cried, and cried and cried. And when the Bible says that someone prayed, it is another thing, a different thing from an actual cry unto the Lord. And the Bible says, someone called, it is another thing still. A talking to God, a crying to God or calling upon God are all different things. When you read that people cried in the Scriptures , the cry is normally a battle cry for a change.

Jacob cried for seven hours, "Unless you bless me, I will not let thee go." What was the angel doing there? He wanted to see whether Jacob would give up easily. Technically, there is no way a man can wrestle with an angel and win in two minutes. The angel may dismantle the whole of his body system in one second. But in the battle there, God wanted to know whether or not Jacob really meant business. He wanted to know whether Jacob would give up.

And as Jacob went on, the angel too must have been praying secretly; although he could not tell Jacob directly, "Don't give up, continue the struggle; don't give up, don't give up." And by the time the fulness of time came, he looked at him and said, "What is thy name?"

Jacob replied, "Jacob".

And the angel said, "Thy name shall not be called Jacob anymore, but you shall be called Israel."

That day, the destiny of Jacob changed. I pray that today will be your day, in the name of Jesus.

So the cry that Jacob cried was because he didn't want to slumber in the tent of his fathers; he wanted to move forward.

The Israelites in Egypt cried unto the Lord: "O Lord, deliver us from the hands of Pharaoh." They were crying for a change.

Somebody like Jabez cried unto the Lord, "O that thou would blest me truly, and thou would excuse me from evil, and thou would enlarge my cost, and keep me away from evil."

The man saw that by his background he was in a big trouble, so he cried for a change and something happened. His life changed.

Elijah was at the celebrated torment at the mount of Carmel with 450 men of the devil and one man of God standing before them. Many of us complain of being persecuted in the house of God but I am yet to see 450 people persecuting one person in any church. And Elijah stood before them and asked them to call upon their god and see if he would answer, and the Lord that answers by fire, let Him be God.

The people of Israel that God delivered from the land of bondage sat down there as spectators while Elijah did all these. Israel had backslided completely. By the way God brought them up they didn't need any Elijah to tell them that God could answer by fire. But that day, all they could do was to look on in amazement, and eventually, Elijah stood and cried unto the God of Israel and Abraham, "Let it be known this day that I am thy prophet, and that I am doing these things at thy word: answer me, O Lord, answer me that these people may know that thou, O Lord, art God, and that thou hath turned their mind back."

And fire fell. What would have happened to Elijah that day if fire did not fall down? That is why I know that, the God that answers by fire is my God.

I am taking you through these cries in the Scripture so that you can see the cries of men who cried unto the Lord because they were not satisfied with the way things were going.

Eventually it got to Elisha. Elisha got to the river of Jordan after Elijah had gone away. The only thing he had was the mantle of Elijah that had fallen unto him. He had to cross the same river; if not, he would be destroyed by terrible creatures by the side of the Jordan river.

His master Elijah had a portion of power and yet, with that portion, Jezebel drove him into wilderness. Elisha knew that, if he was going to survive, he needed more than what Elijah had. The fellow cried for a change. He held up the same mantle and cried, "Where is the Lord God of Elijah?" And the striking of that Jordan represented a change in his life completely.

There was another man in the Bible called Zerubabel. He too uttered a cry unto the Lord. His cry was this: "Who art thou o great mountain? Before Zerubabel, thou shall become a plain." This can be personalised to reflect your situation. And what happened after Zerubabel's cry? The mountain became a plain before Zerubabel.

When Jesus arrived at the tomb of Lazarus He did not raise up His hand and begin to beg. He spoke to His Father in adoration, quietly and reverently. The voice which He too spoke to His Father had changed by the time He turned to the tomb. He spoke to His Father in adoration and thereafter uttered a cry, "Lazarus, come forth." And, quickly the man came. Why did Jesus have to raised His voice now? It was because He was praying for a change of spiritual position. He wanted a man withdrawn from the spirit world back into his natural body and the body to be made whole once again, and for the prison wardens of the gate of heaven to release Lazarus. For these, Jesus had to make a cry.

It is amazing that there could be somebody whose benefit could be in the grave and only for ice cream prayer to be prayed for such a person.

The same cry was what blind Bartemeus raised because he wanted a change. He was tired of begging for alms to survive. He was tired of being rescued from the gutter each time he fell there. So he cried unto the Lord. That is the kind of cry you need to make to obtain the desired change in your life.

Beloved, the truth is this. You either change or you harden. No change is made without some inconvenience. There must be some inconvenience somewhere. You may not like it, but it is that change that will bring you progress. Only the dead man or a very foolish man would not change. Change itself is the very essence of life. To resist change is to resist life itself.

Form the many messages that you must have heard or read, all God is telling you is that He wants a change. Some changes may occur that many of us are not willing to embrace. A lot of people want to stick to their familiar past. If you must stick to your familiar past then forget your future.

If, as a driver, instead of looking through your windscreen you keep looking at your back view mirror, you will certainly crash the vehicle. Even if you are not driving a vehicle but you insist on seeing everybody coming behind you, while you want to move forward, it means you have to turn your head to the back; and if you keep moving forward with you head to the back, you will soon stumble and possibly harm yourself.

A lot of believers are so afraid of venturing into untravelled territories, and many stubbornly cling to dead, old habits. Some cling to old childhood friends that have misguided their lives up to this level. Some cling to the kind of people who have demoted their lives. The Bible says, "Move with the wise and you shall be wise. Move with the foolish and you shall be foolish."

You must make a decision that you want to make change. You must examine all those old habits and practices. Examine all your old friends. Sit down somewhere quiet and aks yourself what each person in your life has contributed to your life. Has he or she added to me or subtracted from me? You must challenge all those old traditions that have yielded nothing to you.

Has your father has bought a pew in the church, with your family name on it? And you tie a high head-wear on Sunday and take your position in it without knowing that you are just cooking yourself? And when trouble comes, you start running around for deliverance; and after finishing the deliverance you go back to your father's seat in your father's church where they apply newer weapons on you, then you run back again?

How long will you slumber in the tent of your fathers? The tent that was not comfortable for your fathers, why do you want to remain there. Remember, beloved, a seed does not take roots until it falls to the ground. If a person decides to keep all his seeds in his hand and keeps resisting change, he is sure to remain with just the number of seeds he holds on to.

I want you to know beloved, that when you look at the sky, you will notice that the stars will not shine until the darkest hour. So if you are a member of MFM and you attend our prayer meetings regularly and you keep saying you are always what you were, you are to be pitied. It means you don't want to change; such a person is a fool of mighty magnitude. It is like somebody standing in the water and keeps breeding mosquitoes in his mind.

Once God is calling you for a change and you refuse to change, He will bombard you in all areas, and when the bombardments come, you will keep shouting, "Hindrance, hindrance, clear out of the way!" But the hindrance will say, "Mr Man, in the name of Jesus," the hindrance will tell you that, that very name you mentioned was the name that put it in your way.

When a life is a changed, a world will change. To go from where you are now, to where God wants you to go, a change is needed. Lack of change is what produces talented but unsuccessful men. Changing just one thing about your life can completely change your whole life.

Many of us need to pray to ask God to get a very good padlock for our mouth. Because once God closes that mouth for you, you will move forward by fire. That was how the Lord had to close the mouth of Zachariah. The man was talking absolute rubbish. A person can talk himself out of his breakthroughs. The little change that God may be asking you to make may be to put a guard in your mouth.

For most of us, all He may be asking of us is to be Bible addicts, and when you drop that flimsy excuse that your brain can hardly hold anything, read the Bible, and decide to change, you will be surprised what the Lord will do for you.

Although you cannot change your biological inheritance, you can change your spiritual inheritance. You can get out of that evil tent that caged your parents. Look at the industries, many of them are closing down in so many areas. When you get to some areas abroad, you will see the remains of once-successful industry which has closed down. Their main problem was that they refused to change.

Change means movement, and movement means friction. What I have found out in my years of counselling is that, it is easier for many people to cry than to change. Women who keep their mouths shut hardly get beaten up.

The change may be difficult, but it is often essential for survival. We cannot become what we seek to become by remaining where we are, The change should start, and the day you finish changing it is that day you are finished.

To slumber in the tent of your father, beloved, is to stagnate. If you do not change, you would not grow.

Sometime ago, I went to the town where I had my primary school. The place was as we left it. I am sure if you enter the classrooms, you will still find all those small seats we sat on when we were six years old. And if I decide to still sit on those seats now, would I be comfortable?

Therefore, there must be a change.

The world hates changes, yet it is the only thing that brings progress. When people come to Mountain of Fire and Miracles Ministries, one of the first things that change in their lives is their prayer life, and by the time a small thing changes in their prayer life, all other things start moving.

When the enemy wants to finish a person, the first area he attacks is his prayer life. Once he takes that out of the way, all the person's shout of superiority over the devil is a mere waste of time.

Progress is impossible without a change. The only human institution where nothing changes is the cemetery. Many resist changes, some tolerate it while some embrace it. If you do not cry out for change this day, you will remain in your chains.

Perhaps you have looked at your life and discovered it is limited, confronted, harassed, attacked, diseased, you need to cry for a change.

May be you are a horizontal person whose main concern in the church is to backbite and spread rumours. Horizontal people normally remain where they are while vertical people move towards God and always move forward. You must cry out for a change today so that you will not be like a person seeking to collect milk from a dead cow or someone who has registered in the school of stagnancy, or someone who covers up a mouth sore or wound with lipstick. Only you can cry out for a change, nobody can do it on your behalf.

If you cry and things change, then your life becomes different. But if things do not change, you are sure to remain the same. If you have hatred for change, it is the architect of decay. That is why some of my favourite songs that I have been singing for a long time is:

Do something new in my life, something new in my life, something new in my life, today. Do something new in my life, something new in my life today.

That song says you want a change. Perhaps you are still one of those people still waving their rosary at the village serpent, and the serpent is swallowing up your rosary and you keep wondering what is happening, or you are one of those people who are as educated as you are, but who still leave their car and walk barefoot to the church?

Or you are one of those people who have been ordained

out of salvation and given a big post to take you out of your destiny, and you keep rejoicing that you are this and that. You may need to cry out to the Lord in order to know where you are.

If you have been experiencing lame breakthroughs, cry out to the Lord now. If you have seen yourself inside an evil family pattern, cry out to the Lord now. If you know that your names are being circulated around evil altars, you need to cry to the Lord now. If you know that your accounts are dead, the enemy has breathed the spirit of death upon it, cry out to the Lord.

Perhaps you have been suffering from what is called prayer paralysis, you need to cry out for a change. Perhaps you have been suffering from evil diversion, you have foreign benefits but have been captured, you have been trapped in the fowler's net, you need to cry out for a change now. Perhaps you have been living in disillusionment, you need to cry out to the Lord for a change.

Sometimes, all that is required for a breakthrough is just a little change in life. What many people call problems are often trumpet calls for a change. After God has used several avenues to talk to a person without obtaining any tangible response from the person, what He does next, is to personally resist such a person, like He did to Adam, Balaam, and Jonah.

Failure in now befalling the experts. The person who thought he was smart is now being outsmarted. The liar is now being outlined. God may just be asking for a change. He wants you to change. He wants areas of your life to change. God is calling for that today.

Perhaps you are at present dissatisfied with all this feeling of being resisted, you have the feeling of frustration, of being useless, being aimless, or being wasted, you know that you are intelligent but nobody is asking to use your brain, and you are being discouraged because of that; or you know that, right now, as you are, the enemy is the one dancing all over the garden of your life, you need to cry out to the Lord now, tell Him that you need a change, that you need to open up the garden of your life to the Holy Spirit, that you must take action against all unchristlike attitude in your life.

You must cry to the Lord that all He has been telling you, you want to do them one hundred percent. God has a job to do, He has provided men and women who will do the job. If you are privilege to be one of those He has put in positions to do the job, and one way or the other, He is calling for a change in your life, but you keep resisting, He will raise up a stone. He cannot leave a vacuum in His programme. No one is indispensable in the work of God. If you think you are the most talented person in the universe, God can create a new person, put more talents in Him and send him down, just to disgrace your pride.

Many people are following the pattern in the tent of their fathers. If you are reading this book, and you know that you have not given your life to Christ, I advise you to do so quickly now so that you can get a prompt response to your cry to the Lord today.

What God showed to me before writing this chapter is that, there are millions of people walking behind their breakthroughs. This means that, the breakthroughs should have been in their hands but those breakthroughs walk past them because of certain changes they have refused to make.

The day you begin to pray the correct prayers, correct things will begin to happen. Do not worry about those witches that have been following you around; when they all die one by one, they will leave you alone. Do not worry about the people who have threatened your life. When God padlocks their power they will leave you alone. But for God to do these things, He has certain things for you too to do. if your spiritual hands are weak and you want to carry a big thing, and the Lord keeps telling you, "Son, add this strength to your hands first," but you keep resisting that power into your hands, you are walking away from your breakthroughs.

The Lord has provided us with table in the presence of the enemy of most of us, unfortunately, they keep scattering the table with their own legs. This is very sad.

As you read this, confess your inadequacies to the Lord; tell Him you are sorry. In many areas, God wants you to change, you keep resisting Him? You had better tell Him to forgive you, so that you can move forward immediately. Promise the Lord you will change, no matter which area of your life He wants you to change. Ask Him to forgive you, that you will start changing as from now on. If He has been complaining about the temperature of your prayer, ask Him to forgive you.

PRAYER POINTS

1. O ye that troubles my Israel, my God shall trouble you henceforth, in the name of Jesus.
2. Every generational spirit, reporting my past to my future, depart now, in the name of Jesus.
3. Every dark power, working against my family, what are waiting for, die, in the name of Jesus.
4. O God that delivered Daniel from the lion's den, deliver me by fire, in the name of Jesus.
5. Where is the Lord God of Elijah? Manifest Your power in my destiny, in the name of Jesus.
6. Every witchcraft stagnation of my progress, die, in the name of Jesus.
7. I need a divine change by fire, in the name of Jesus.
8. Hear the voice of the Living God, you my destiny and change to the best, in the name of Jesus.
9. I shall not slumber, in the tent of my fathers, in the name of Jesus.
10. You powers in the heavenlies, listen to my prophecies, I need a change by fire, in the name of Jesus.
11. Anti-success witchcraft, die, in the name of Jesus.

12. Every cage in my father's house, die, in the name of Jesus.
13. By the power that changed the life of Jabez, let my life change, in the name of Jesus.
14. (Raise your hands to the heavenlies) Any power that says these hands will not prosper, die, in the name of Jesus.
15. The power of the idols of my father's house, hear the word of the Living God, I am not your candidate, therefore, die, in the name of Jesus.

Chapter 3

YOUR DESTINY AND HOUSEHOLD WITCHCRAFT

Three issues are tied to the topic of this chapter: Destiny, Household and Witchcraft.

What is destiny?

- ☞ This is God's purpose for your life, it is your appointed or ordained future.
- ☞ It is what God has pre-determined you to be or which you have become.

It is for this reason that the enemy can be defined as any spirit, power or personality that would not allow you to fulfil divines destiny for your life.

- ☞ It is the reason why you were born.

If there is a power that does not wish for you to fulfil the purpose of which you were born, it is not a matter to be taken lightly.

- ☞ It is what God had in mind before He created you and sent you down here.
- ☞ It is what He has written down for you in His book of life.

Several times we hear our Lord Jesus Christ talking

about His destiny. Then at one time, He said, the Son of man goeth as it is written. And if any power does not want you to go as it is written of you, it means such a power as re-written your book. This is the reason the Bible speaks of contrary handwritings.

The second word that emerges from the title is "household".

What is household?

- This is the domestic unit containing member of your family living together.
- Household means lines of ancestors.
- It could also mean those who dwell under the same roof.
- It could also mean the living places or possession belonging to such a unit.

So the term 'household' covers so many things.

Briskly, we shall take a look at the last word, which is 'witchcraft'.

What is witchcraft?

☞ This is the legal arm of satan, the arm of destruction; the power of the enemy to do and undo.

This is, therefore, why one of the most beautiful verses in the Bible is where Jesus came to 'undo' the worked of the enemy.

CASES OF ACTIVITIES OF HOUSEHOLD WICKEDNESS IN THE SCRIPTURES

We shall quickly look at the same Scriptures. In Genesis 4:8, we read:

And Cain talked with Abel his brother: and it came to pass, when they were in the field, that Cain rose up against Abel his brother, and slew him.

The above is the first example of household wickedness. Here were two brothers who came out of the same womb. And when we go into Genesis 37:23-24 we read:

And it came to pass, when Joseph was come unto his brethren, that they stript Joseph out of his coat, *his* coat of *many* colours that *was* on him;
24And they took him, and cast him into a pit: and the pit *was* empty, *there was* no water in it.

Who were the people who did this to Joseph? His own brothers. Read verse 25. I pray that any power celebrating evil against you shall be disgraced, in Jesus' name.

And they sat down to eat bread: and they lifted up their eyes and
looked, and, behold, a company of Ishmeelites came from Gilead with
their camels bearing spicery and balm and myrrh, going to carry *it* down
to Egypt. 26 And Judah said unto his brethren, What profit *is it* if we slay
our brother, and conceal his blood? 27 Come, and let us sell him to the
Ishmeelites, and let not our hand be upon him; for he *is* our brother *and*
our flesh. And his brethren were content. 28 Then there passed by
Midianites merchantmen; and they drew and lifted up Joseph out of the
pit, and sold Joseph to the Ishmeelites for twenty *pieces* of silver: and
they brought Joseph into Egypt.

In the book of numbers 12:1-3, we find:

And Miriam and Aaron spake against Moses because of the Ethiopian
woman whom he had married: for he had married an Ethiopian woman.
2 And they said, Hath the LORD indeed spoken only by Moses? hath he not
spoken also by us? And the LORD heard *it*. 3 (Now the man Moses *was* very
meek, above all the men which *were* upon the face of the earth.)

Ignorance is a terrible thing, it is the mother of personal destruction. A little of ignorance can destroy things forever.

It is important, therefore, to know that there is a spirit behind household wickedness. That is the spirit we should seek to arrest.

As it can be seen in the story of Joseph above, God had

a special purpose for his life; indeed, the reason you are still alive today is not that there are no powers that would have wanted you gone, but because God has a purpose for your life. Obviously, it is not normal when a person takes the youngest boy in the family and decides he must die.

In the life Moses too, we see household wickedness in operation. Who was Mariam? She was the woman who took Moses out of the water. And who was Aaron? Aaron, of course, was his older brother; these two people now joined together to speak against Moses, but we thank God that he intervened.

Judges 15:9-12:

Then the Philistines went up, and pitched in Judah, and spread
themselves in Lehi. [10]And the men of Judah said, Why are ye come up
against us? And they answered, To bind Samson are we come up, to do to
him as he hath done to us. [11]Then three thousand men of Judah went to
the top of the rock Etam, and said to Samson, Knowest thou not that the
Philistines *are* rulers over us? what *is* this *that* thou hast done unto us?
And he said unto them, As they did unto me, so have I done unto them.
[12]And they said unto him, We are come down to bind thee, that we may
deliver thee into the hand of the Philistines. And Samson said unto them,
Swear unto me, that ye will not fall upon me yourselves.

So the brethren of Samson, too, came to bind Samson. Another case of household wickedness.

Judges 16:6:

And Delilah said to Samson, Tell me, I pray thee, wherein thy great strength *lieth*, and wherewith thou mightest be bound to afflict thee.

Samson had just married a fire extinguisher, and there was the woman asking her husband where his great power lied so that she could torment his life. After all, the woman did not hide her intention.

If you are a pastor and your wife confronts you with a request to destroy you, I am sure the first thing you would say is that the woman needs deliverance.

2 Samuel 15:13:

And Absalom said unto him, See, thy matters *are* good and right; but *there is* no man *deputed* of the king to hear thee.

Here was another case of household wickedness - with David running away from his own son.

And when we go into the book of Job 2:9 we see Job not realizing that he was in the center of competition where the angels were hailing him to carry on and the devil begging for him to be tested so that he might fall. His wife, too, did not know all this.

Then said his wife unto him, Dost thou still retain thine integrity? curse God, and die.

It was his wife's ploy to marry another person. Just as we have wicked husbands, so we have wicked wives.

Now, in the book of Micah 7:6, we read:

For the son dishonoureth the father, the daughter riseth up against her mother, the daughter in law against her mother in law; a man's enemies *are* the men of his own house.

The Great Wall of China is highly protective that enemies could not penetrate it. The first time enemies succeeded in penetrating the Great wall was when the guards accepted a bribe. These tallies with a Yoruba proverb that says if the household death does not kill one, the one outside will have problems doing so.

Jesus strikes the nail on the head in Matthew 10:36 when He says:

And a man's foes *shall be* they of his own household.

I have brought out all these points about household wickedness as contained in the Bible so that we can understand this.

LIFE CASES

It remains one issue that is not clear to many people.

When we were in school, we had a very brilliant boy. On prize giving days, it was usual for him to go with all the available prizes. The lowest mark he ever got in Mathematics was either 96 or 95. If he was given five questions and asked to answer three, he would answer the three and still go ahead to answer the other two, just for the fun.

When this boy finished his school certificate, he made 'A"s in seven papers; soon, he sat for his advanced level examination, come out in flying colours and proceeded to oversees.

When he was leaving, members of his family organized a very big party for him. Just as they were adding him to the airport, his younger sister moved close to him and whispered into his ears and asked him to choose between the overseas he was going and his life. The boy was surprised. Anyway, because alcohol was freely served at the party organized for him, he thought the girl probably drank too much of it.

Our friend made his way abroad, did excellently well there, securing first class in his course. One week to the graduation ceremony, however, he went to a swimming pool.

He got on the diving board and leaped from there. For some strange reasons, however, his feet slipped in the water. He smashed his head on the concrete floor of the swimming pool. His brain went one way and his smashed skull went the other way. The breaking of his head was so much that he was brought to Nigeria headless.

When the corpse arrived at the airport, that younger sister was the one rolling on the floor, crying her heart out. The boy's enemies had already finished their agenda.

Joseph's brother put him in the pit and started eating. Every time I think about this, I feel like crying.

Some week's back, I saw someone at our 'Prayer Rain' programme giving testimony. I looked at her closely and discovered it was that brilliant boy's younger sister; she is now born again. She had gone through deliverance and had become free. And the mystery of our faith is that, having done all these, the Lord would accept her, even though that our friend is gone.

At a revival some years back, a little girl was holding the coat of our revivalist, asking him to deliver her for she did not want to be alone in the world. The revivalist asked what the problem was. She told the man that they were four in her family; the first born was a medical doctor, the second one a lawyer, the third one had a hunchback while she was the fourth child. She told the revivalist that she had been asked to bring the medical doctor. She had already taken the doctor there and he had been eaten. Likewise, the lawyer too was asked for; she took him there and was in the like manner eaten. The curious thing is that not even the lawyer's many degree could save him; he and his other brother died in mysterious circumstances.

The little girl got scared when the hunch-backed brother was requested for. "I don't want to be alone in this world; please, deliver me," said the sister. The revivalist was shocked. He asked the girl if her brothers that have been eaten up were not the ones paying her school fees. The girl said yes, and that since all these brothers had died, she had nobody to pay her fees.

Many things we say at the MFM are not clear to many people. For example, when we say a particular power should die, this baffles so many people. When you carefully check your Scriptures, you will find out that it is not always that God pronounces a death sentence on anyone, but when it comes to the matter of witchcraft, the Bible says God's death sentence is upon them. And there is a reason. So this explains why we always ask certain powers to die.

Of course, we know that spirits do not die, but when we say, 'die', the meaning of this is very simple. It means that they should become functionless, useless and unavailable. You can't find somebody who could bring a corpse to the altar for marriage with it because that corpse no longer function as a human being. So when we ask them to die, it means we remove their function.

Jesus wanted to do that to some spirits, but those spirits started begging him to leave them alone. They knew that once Jesus dealt with them, they would cease tormenting human beings. So when we say that the power of witchcraft should die, it means that anytime they gather to do something against you, it would not work. Why? It is because the power is dead to work against you..

MONITORING AND REPORTING AGENTS

In every family with potentials, there is a destroyer. In practically all families, there is, at least, one agent of destruction.

David called them strange children and asked God to

deliver him from strange children. Why should David say this kind of prayer? This is because a sixty-year-old woman who has been to the maternity ward five to six times has some element of compassion in her, but for a child who is asked to kill or torment any member of the family, she would have no compassion in her in carrying out the orders given her in evil forces. This accounts David's prayer to be delivered from strange children.

There is a monitoring and reporting agent in all families, unless that family does not have potentials. This could even mean that the enemy has finished work on the family and there is no one again rising up.

Everyone has a case file in the spirit world. Some people's files have been passed many agents of darkness. This is why we don't pray against human beings when we say witches in the family should die, what such witches do at the point of death is to transfer the case file. But when we say that the power behind the witches should die, that power becomes untransferable.

Beloved, you need power to dismantle close enemies. The lamentations of many can be found in the word of Jesus. In psalm 41:9 says:

Yea, mine own familiar friend, in whom I trusted, which did eat of my bread, hath lifted up *his* heel against me.

What can be more ironic than this? There is a Chinese proverb which says, "O Lord, deal with my friends, I shall take care of my enemies." The implication of this is that an enemy has, at least, declared himself as an enemy and has been identified as such, but a friend whom you don't know can be terrible. It is very difficult for you to dodge a stone thrown at you from the back of your head.

The satanic agenda for many of us started right from the womb, and many people suffer from that womb to the grave and are never able to fulfil their destiny.

The destinies of most black people have been buried alive by satanic relatives. From now, beloved, every destiny destroyer must be hunted down and dealt with. The deeper the satanic hook a person has swallowed has gone, the more difficult it is to dislodge it.

Take, for example, a person who was born in a polygamous home where there are about eight wives, his own mother as the number fifth wife. In that same home, food is freely shared and, with it, witchcraft is being transferred or passed round. When that person has partaken in the eating of such bewitched food, enemy's agenda has already been concluded in his life.

HOUSEHOLD WICKEDNESS

The phrase, "household wickedness" is still vague to many people. But I shall give some definitions.

Resident Wickedness

First, there is what we call resident wickedness. This has been in the family before the birth of the victim and, as such, he has no control over it just in the same way we have no control or say in the matter of who should be our father or mother. This means that, long before you were born, your mother or your father was already a witch wizard.

One day a father called all the children together to announce a special decree that none of them should be greater than he was. He warned that, should anyone of them try it, he would die. Secondly, he decreed that none of them should have another wife than the one he would give them.

While all of them complied with his decree, there was a

particular one who was born again, even though he remained lukewarm in the spirit. He got up and told the father frankly that he would marry only the partner given him by God. The old man did not argue with him.

So, all the other sons took the wives brought to them by the father from the village. Even though a wife was kept in the village for the born again brother, he never went there to take the wife, instead he took for a wife he met in Lagos. And, funny though, he turned out to be the only prosperous son of the man. His prosperity soared to the extent that he overshadowed the father.

All of a sudden, however, the wife cried from her sleep one night, "Daddy, daddy, leave me, leave me," before her husband could reach her, she had given up the ghost. And immediately the woman died, the brother's fortune went till he became a pauper.

The day the young man came to see me, he cried like a baby. Even as I write this, I can still remember his cry. He kept lamenting, "A dear, loving wife." The woman was a victim of resident wickedness.

Acquired Wickedness

Secondly, there is acquired wickedness. This happen

when kids accept sweets and biscuits from their mates at school. When such kids return home, they become something else. This always marks the beginning of a serious battle in the house.

Sometimes ago, I listened to a couple who said their little boy of about seven years woke them up at about two mid-night to tell the mother that her womb and breast had been put under the water by him. Turning to the father, the boy said the man's money in the bank had been hung on top of a tree. The fact that the father already had a 'bank' on top of a tree was responsible for his financial failure.

The couple asked the boy what he meant by these and he told them point blank that if they could not understand all he was saying, they should go and ask their pastor. When the shocked parents asked the boy why he should be doing all this to them, he said it was not his fault. "My friends in the school took me there," said the boy.

Tormenting Wickedness

Thirdly, there is tormenting wickedness. This is the situation where the enemy has no plan to stay in the family, only witches to torment, punish, oppress and go away. This, nonetheless, is a brand of household wickedness.

There was a brother who was a found at making friends. As a result, he knew so many people from whom he could easily take references to win contracts, but he never won any contract. This frustrated him, and he went to consult a very senior herbalist. After the herbalist consulted his oracle, he told the man that even if he went to collect references from ten heads of state, there was no way he could make any headway.

What this translated into was that if he was the head of his household and he continued to live in hunger, the other members of the family would automatically live in hunger, too.

Attacking Wickedness

Fourthly, there is attacking wickedness. Even though this stays outside the family and only comes in to punish the victim, it is still household wickedness.

Current Family Initiation

Fifthly, there is the current family initiation. This can be conscious or unconscious and members get initiated on regular basis. And if any member of your family is being recruited, whether or not you are aware of it, it is still household witchcraft.

Past and Current Infiltration

Marital Wickedness

Seven, there is marital wickedness. When you think you've got married to the right man, but this same man still has strange women outside in the name of wives, those strange women represent household wickedness because all the information about you as his wife and his children would be divulged to the strange women by the man. When two people get married, it means two families have fused together, thus establishing a larger ground in which many forces can operate.

Wickedness by Consultation

There is also wickedness by consultation. If there is any member of your family who is still going round her herbalists, witch-doctors and fetish priests, it is still the same household witchcraft.

Polluted Family Houses

Ninth, there are polluted family houses. Many of those places we call family houses are places where destinies are being destroyed regularly. It is also what we call magnetic witchcraft. Many people stay in such families and are unable to prosper until they leave. Some foolish one's too stay and fight over what they call there inheritance. Isn't it better for such people to pray to God to give them their own property?

Delegated Strongman in Families

Evil Assistance

Eleventh, we have what is called evil assistance. This happens when your unbelieving parents desire to help you by consulting witchcraft on your behalf to help you solve some problems.

Revenge Witchcraft

There is also the 'revenge witchcraft'. A person is annoyed with you, but doesn't know how to go about it; he or she consequently obtains witchcraft to deal with you.

Property Possession

Thirteenth, we have the 'property possession'. In this case, witchcraft is employed in taking a property belonging to a group of people.

Parasitic Witchcraft

Lastly, there is also what can be referred to as parasitic witchcraft. This happens, where there is a family set-up into which a house-help or a total stranger is brought into that family. This outsider then embarks on a systematical destruction of the family.

A top person in the society, a governor to be precise, one day suddenly heard the agonising cry of his daughter and ran there. What he saw shocked him into the marrow. It was his house-boy trying to rape his daughter. In annoyance, he reached for his gun and chased out the house-boy.

Beloved, how do you fight the person who beared you in her womb for nine months? How do you fight a person who knows everything about you? How do you fight a person who handled your placenta ? How do you fight that person who gave you your first bath? How do you fight a person who knows your weakness and strengths?

How do you fight a person who has been feeding you with poison for the past twenty years? How do you fight a person who is your own offspring? How do you fight the person who collected your dowry? Or that person who has assisted you to host your engagement?

You will have to deal with the power behind those evil forces around you.

WORKS OF HOUSEHOLD WITCHCRAFT

It is the anointing of this household witchcraft that has led to what is called internal burial. This means that memories and ideas are not allowed to come to life. All these are buried at the unconscious level; all those things that could have made the person prosper have been buried inside of him by the power of the household witchcraft.

Household witchcraft is responsible for the animal instinct that leads a forty-year-old man to rape a two-year-old girl. There, of course, must be something strange behind it.

It is also household witchcraft that is behind what is called a scape-clothing which makes a man to always look for someone else to misdirect his anger to whenever anything goes wrong.

Household witchcraft invades people's dream to present the person's enemy as his friend, and vice versa. This makes the victim to begin to fire his arrow in the wrong direction. While the real enemies continue to have a field day.

They are the ones responsible for the substitution of virtues, giving the servant the horse and make the owner of the virtue to trudge along all his life.

They are the ones responsible for the forces of resistance that keep pushing the person away from where he should prosper.

They are the one responsible for evil transfer of ones person's virtue to another.

Also, they are the ones responsible for personality disorder and the evil pressure some people are feeling all around them that make them do what a normal person should not do.

They are the ones responsible for the blockages, the dead-end syndrome, the paralysis and sending confusing information to people.

They are the ones that eliminate people in their prime.

DIVINE ANSWER

The Bible has only one answer for witchcraft spirit and powers of witchcraft. He hates them with perfect hatred and wants to have nothing to do with them, and the sentence God has issued against them is death!

And if God has passed the death sentence on witchcraft agents and practitioners, whether African, black or white, the death hangs on them.

The Bible condemns all these evil forces with serious condemnation and it says, "Say ye to the wicked, It shall be ill with him."

There were five sisters in a family. After getting married, each of them was sent back to their father's house. However, there was one of them who resolved that her own marriage was not going to be like the others.

Somebody gave her a copy of our book "Pray Your Way to Breakthrough", started coming to our meetings and praying. The first night she prayed, the grandmother who lived in the house called her and asked her what sort of prayer she had resorted to these days.

"Aren't you an Anglican anymore? Why not return to

that kind of gentle prayers you used to pray before?"

Said the grandmother.

The next day, the sister did another 30-minutes hot session of prayer. The granny called her again to caution her against killing anyone with her new prayers.

The next day, the sister intensifies her prayers, this time making it last for three hours! The following morning, the granny did not wake up. When they looked under granny's bed amid all her things there, there was a small strange looking padlock. They brought out the padlock. While the other sisters could only stare at the padlock, the 'praying-sister' suggested that they should break the padlock.

When the padlock was broken, they found a small piece of paper inside it with a blood-stained-cotton-wool. On the small piece of paper were the names of the five sisters. The sister poured anointing oil on the padlock and burnt it to ashes. The following day, her own husband came to take her home.

At this juncture, let me ask you a question.

Do you like to fulfil your destiny? Do you have a

conviction in your heart that you are not where you are supposed to be?

Many of us are looking for the enemy outside while the enemy is inside, either inherited, acquired, infiltration, attack, etc. In fact, the rate at which small boys and girls confess to witchcraft these days is alarming.

After praying the prayer points at the end of this chapter, don't be surprised when you hear that some people in your village have started confessing to witchcraft.

The only thing that can hinder your prayer is unrepentant syndrome. You can't fight darkness while darkness is in you. Ask the Lord for forgiveness. And if you have any sin at all, confess it to the Lord.

Likewise, if you are reading this, but have not surrendered your life to Christ, you had better do so now. If you belong to this category, all you have to do is close your eyes and say the following prayers.

"Fathers, in the name of Jesus, I come before You this day; come into my life, Lord Jesus, in Jesus' name I pray. Amen."

PRAYER POINTS

1. Every mother of witchcraft in my family, what are you waiting for? Die, in the name of Jesus.
2. Every evil spirit of "I have to do it", in my family, die, in the name of Jesus.
3. Any power eating my food and drinking my water but planning for my destruction, loose your power, in the name of Jesus.
4. Thou resident wickedness in my family, die, in the name of Jesus.
5. Every padlock of witchcraft, in my family, burn up, in the name of Jesus.
6. Every witchcraft hand, that carried me as a baby, break, in the name of Jesus.
7. You mountain of darkness, hindering my progress, die, in the name of Jesus.
8. Every plantation of witchcraft on my father's side, what are you waiting for? Die, in the name of Jesus.
9. Every seed of witchcraft on my mother's side,

what are you waiting for? Die, in the name of Jesus.

10. Every strange child in my family, loose your power, in the name of Jesus.
11. By the power that broke the yoke of Pharaoh with strong hand, inherited witchcraft, die, in the name of Jesus.
12. Every owner of witchcraft load, carry your load away from my family, in the name of Jesus.
13. Every herbalist, consulted against me, I command your power to disgrace you, in the name of Jesus.
14. Every witchcraft embargo, on my finances, die, in the name of Jesus.

Chapter 4

THE TRAGEDY OF FOUNDATIONAL WITCHCRAFT

FAULTY FOUNDATION

It is a great tragedy, to know that most people are suffering greatly not for their own sins but for the sins of their ancestors.

Many lives have been ruined and are still being ruined because of the wicked and ungodly lives led by their ancestors. Unfortunately, many Christians are in this category; they fast, pray, cast out, bind and loose, yet nothing happens.

Now close your eyes and pray this prayer point.

My glory wherever you are, arise, sit-up and refuse to be silent, in the name of Jesus.

The major cause of this stagnancy is the faulty foundation of witchcraft, idolatry, occultism and idol worship laid by the ancestors.

I thank the Lord for the opportunity to share this message with you and I pray that s you read on, your eyes of understanding will be opened, and you will be empowered to fight a good warfare.

Close your eyes and say this to the heavenlies with your

right raise up.

Oh thou that troubleth my Israel, my God shall trouble you today, in the name of Jesus.

From the title, we can pick out three key words. Tragedy, foundation and witchcraft.

WHAT IS A TRAGEDY?

- The word tragedy in itself means an evil happening or occurrence that has a devastating effect on the victim.

At times, it may be so terrible as to claim lives and property.

Physical and spiritual tragedy

Tragedy can be examined from two perspectives. Physical and spiritual.

When a man suddenly loses his physical possessions through fire, even at the peak of his professional career, it is a tragedy. When his wife and children suddenly die in one day, it is a tragedy, a great physical tragedy.

On the other hand - and this is worse than the first, is

the spiritual tragedy. Or what do you say has happened to a Christian who used to be on fire for the Lord, but who is now under intense fire of the enemy?

What do you call a situation where by a choirmaster impregnates more than half of the female choristers?

What do you say has happened to a Christian who talks of his Christianity in the past?

WHAT IS A FOUNDATION?

☞ The foundation is that part on which the whole structures rest.

☞ It is that hidden part that anchors deeply in the soil.

The foundation is also the beginning of something - a river, stream, ocean and sea, etc.

Physical and spiritual foundation

Foundation can also be explained physically and spiritually.

On the physical plane, the foundation holds up an entire structure, a house or a stretch of bridge. The beautiful houses that we see are laid on foundations that were dug deep into the ground. When you dig a foundation hole, you then pour in concrete, iron, gravel and other things that will give it strength to carry the load to be placed on it.

Spiritually, the foundation refers to the early beginnings of a life as laid by our ancestors. It refers to that which has become the very first thing to which our spiritual lives have been anchored.

These foundations, physical or spiritual, can be faulty, which if not taken care of, will lead to destruction. Unfortunately, most people have their spiritual foundations in wicked practices and that is why persistent troubles and problems plague many people.

Complicated issues

A lot of bad foundations have become negatively strengthened as a result of marriage. A man with witchcraft practices in his background got married to a woman with occultic practices as her family legacy, what do you think can or will happen to the children of such a marriage?

A life built on a faulty foundation can only bring forth bad fruits. Why should the Lord answer you when your name, *Esubiyi, Oguntola, Oguntolu,* and *Osunbiyi,* still reflects and glorifies idols?

How can the Lord answer you when the cause of the faulty foundation is still standing in place?

Why should you progress when someone in your family was responsible for another person's stagnancy?

Close your eyes and pray this prayer point. *I challenge the foundations of my life with the blood of Jesus and fire of the Holy Ghost, in Jesus' name.*

WHAT IS WITCHCRAFT?

This is best defined from the Scriptures.

Exodus 22:18:

Thou shalt not suffer a witch to live.

There are very few offences in the Bible that the Lord commands death upon the offender and the verse above is an example. The question is this: Why should the Lord want a witch killed?

Deuteronomy 18:10:

There shall not be found among you *any one* that maketh his son or his daughter to pass through the fire, or that useth divination, *or* an observer of times, or an enchanter, or a witch,

Verses 11 and 12 of the same chapter tell us what the Lord does to such people.

The Lord hates, and with perfect hatred too, these things and they are abominations unto Him. This explains why God may command death on all the inhabitants of a land and still go ahead to order a total destruction of the town by putting to death everything that has breath and destroy all buildings.

Leviticus 20:27:

A man also or woman that hath a familiar spirit, or that is a wizard, shall surely be put to death: they shall stone them with stones: their blood *shall be* upon them.

Isaiah 8:19:

And when they shall say unto you, Seek unto them that have familiar spirits, and unto wizards that peep, and that mutter: should not a people seek unto their God? for the living to the dead?

These verses we have read have a central theme- the Lord abhors witchcraft and they that practise it, which is why His judgement is death.

It is not enough for you to just read this and put down

the book, but read it, get violent in your spirit and pray violently so that your foundation and you may be corrected.

Activities of witchcraft

Beloved, it is a terrible thing to have witches in the family, it is an abomination on which the Lord has passed a sentence of death.

If the judgement of the Lord on witchcraft and witches is death, why then do people still practise it? What are the gains and benefits?

What is the sense in eating their own children and those of other people? Why place the lives of people on hold? Why destroy their help of the future to come?

It is all foolishness, a load of total foolishness indeed.

Now, how many children of witches make progress to win scholarships, live good lives or travel abroad? The god of this world has covered their eyes with foolishness.

It is this their foolishness that makes the Lord to abhor them so much that He wants them dead. The Lord knows them, their activities and their sources of power, heavens, sun, moon and stars.

Witches have no tangible emotion and this explains why any child of theirs that refuses to play their game would be dealt with seriously. Because of their subtle and cunning ways, they have been able to penetrate into the church and introduce many horrible things.

Another point is that, if a church is really the church of God, they would come around to fight it.

Witchcraft has a twin-sister called prostitution. This explains why you find scantily dressed ladies in dark and lonely places, especially at night, looking for men and any unfortunate man is destroyed.

These witches destroy altars of God, just like Jezebel, they cause disobedience, steal the word of God from people's hearts, use invisible powers to cause havoc and issue curses, whether playfully or seriously, and these curses will stick.

They are very destructive and have caused untold damage to lives and are still causing damages. They are always blood-thirsty and will always go where they can get free blood.

Many a time they appear to be telling the truth but

these 'truths' are causing untold havoc and damage to countries, people and the world.

I remember the story of a man with three wives. The man died mysteriously and his family cried fowl. They insisted on visiting a occultic priest (*ayelala*) to find the culprit but the first two wives who were very powerful witches confused the demon and diviner such that the third wife was accused of being the killer of their husband.

These forces are so wicked that, you need not to have offended them before they would attack you. You may want to believe that since you don't cross people's path or their paths that they would leave you alone. Then you are absolutely wrong. Just for the fact that you are alive, they will attack you. If you choose to pursue your destiny, there would be troubles and if you are stagnant then you are finished.

Since their major operations are in the night, they believe that their activities are not known, they think their deeds are not seen, they become proud, tell lies, issue curses, multiply armed robbery and increase vices in the society.

They go as far as converting human beings to horses that

upon which they ride to their covens. They sell nations and families. Night and day, they are at work, seeing all that is going on, planning evil and devouring human flesh.

They come in the night as spirit husbands or wives, put terrible marks on people, use cobwebs against the unsuspecting ones and destroy destinies of promising children.

Little wonder the Lord said suffer not a witch to live.

They believe so much in their powers of seduction that they go after men and women of God to pull them down. They work hand in hand with other wicked spirits to perform counterfeit creations.

One of our churches in Port Harcourt Nigeria recorded a strange incident. A woman came for prayers and as the intensity of the prayers increased, a strange thing happened. A male organ came out of her body right there in the presence of her husband.

When they finished praying, the husband said she could not follow him home. A closer examination revealed that they had been married for 16 years and now he wanted to run away, surely whatever was in the woman had been transferred into him and all he needed to do was to pray.

Beloved, all these terrible acts are the handiwork of the witches and an extension of witchcraft powers. They have destroyed and they are still destroying.

Everything you have read so far is based on a research that I have been doing for the past 20 years. I will give more examples, for you to know where we are going.

TRUE LIFE EXAMPLES

Number One

Some year's back, I was travelling to Benin City in the eastern part of Nigeria. As we approached the city, the man sitting beside me suddenly insisted on the bus pulling over for him to ease himself. All entreaties that he would do so at Benin proved futile, when the driver finally stopped, he jumped down and ran into the bush with a carrier bag. By the time he came back, he was dress in rags.

When I questioned him, he said if he wore those nice clothes into his family house that would certainly be his end. When I asked why, he told me that his mother confessed to witchcraft and died, likewise his grandmother, moreover, if you went home at that time, you were not likely to return alive.

The irony of it all is that many of us are from such homes, towns and cities and we have gone back to display our wealth and are now in trouble.

Close your eyes and pray this prayer point.

Every wicked power of my family line, release my destiny, in the name of Jesus.

Number Two

There is also the case of a brother who just got born again when he travelled home. At home, they served him a pounded yam with chicken and *egusi* soup. Ordinarily, he would just have sat down to eat but he decided to pray and as he laid his hand on the food and said, " I sanctify this food, in the name of Jesus." He suddenly heard a cockcrow, and when he looked at his plate, there was a live cock all covered in soup standing in the plate. The brother ran, forgot his travelling bag and boarded a bus coming to Lagos.

He wept bitterly. He now understood why things were not working for him, each meal he had eaten in the past had programmed something into his life.

Why not close your eyes and pray this prayer point.

Every witchcraft food that I have eaten, fire of God, burn them, in the name of Jesus.

Beloved, many people are trouble because of what they had eaten in the camp of the enemy. Some of these things had been eaten years ago and have now come alive in the bodies and they now have developed cancer, ulcer and other strange sicknesses. These are not sicknesses but live animals moving about in their bodies. This is a terrible act of witchcraft.

Number Three

Sometime ago, a man called all his children and told them that if any of them wants to be richer than him, the child would die. This is no joke and he told them that the reason they would die young was because before they were born, he had already gathered their virtues to make him prosperous. As a result, the children were poor while their father was stingingly rich.

Even the professor amongst them used to go and beg the man for money; none of the children could say how they spent their money.

Number Four

Let us take the story of brother Kukunte. His mother was stoned to death after confessing to witchcraft. Brother Kukunte ran to England to study and by the time we met, he had spent 16 years in England and had not succeeded in passing the equivalent of Nigerian School Certificate. He had made no progress at all, he never could hold down a job.

The principle of death kept working in his destiny because the Lord had already passed a death sentence that flowed down. This death sentence would clamp down on the marriage of some, while, for others, it's their prosperity. Some, it is their academics, but something somewhere must be clamped.

Number Five

Another brother Akanka had a similar problem. His father confessed to witchcraft and died thereafter. His mother also confessed to witchcraft but lived. Brother Akanka was very handsome to behold: tall, muscular, well-built, but his legs were useless, not through any accident, they were just useless.

It reminds me of the boy that confessed to witchcraft at the Prayer City; he said he donated his own legs. Brother Akanka's legs had been donated and he would still have been alive today if not for a tragic mistake he made.

One day, he made a journey home and said to his mother, "Mama, come, I want to talk to you," and as she came closer, he bit her ear and began to strangulate her. The villagers rescued her from him. The mother vowed to retaliate; she told him that it is only those that are alive that can bite and strangulate people. To cut a long story short, brother Akanka did not last one week before he died.

If there is witchcraft in your family line, I want you to know that it will affect your life, pollute your destiny and destroy you. This is not a matter of "I am this and that."

Number Six

Sister Tolontolo was initiated at birth through the use of a waistband that must be used for all new born babies. It is the type that is used to wrap them after their first bath.

Sister Tolontolo escaped to England thinking that she was safe but one morning, she woke up and there was not a single hair on her head. In no time, one breast became infected with cancer and they had to remove it. All this while, she was yet to get married. The last time I saw her, the breast was swollen like a giant balloon and she was afraid of going in for another operation because she didn't want to die.

Number Seven

Sister Parontina's case is equally pathetic. She had seven brothers and one sister, all born again and all wretchedly poor. The only rich one was not born again and was a herbalist. Their parents had locked up their destines and only released that of the herbalist because he agreed to join them.

If you are reading this book, you need to pray. If you see people rising then suddenly coming down, check their foundation.

Number Eight

A pastor, Tinco, was put in charge of the first church, it scattered. The congregation reduced to 14 from 200; of the 14, 10 are little children and because they could not pay tithes, the church folded up.

They took him to another church where he impregnated the wife of his driver and he was removed in disgrace. At the third church, a woman drowned while he was conducting baptism by immersion for her.

In Pastor Tinco's family, they worshipped a river deity and this deity dealt with him seriously.

Number Nine

Brother Rondorondo's case is such that, no one dared to walk by his family house in broad daylight; if you did, you will not see the next day. So terrible was it that nobody allowed their daughters to marry any member of their family.

There were five children in that family and brother Rondorondo was the oldest and by far the most educated. He left school after primary 5.

Close your eyes and pray this prayer point: *Every tree covenanting my placenta with witchcraft, die, in the name of Jesus.*

Number Ten

Another brother Kakraka was summoned home because his mother was confessing to witchcraft. As he got home, he was shocked to hear his own mother asking him to forgive her because she was responsible for the deaths of his first and second wives and all his male children. In all she confessed to having killed 103 persons and turning another 35 into armed robbers.

Brother Kakraka's mother had three children, two male and one female. He is the first and you have read his case. The second child presently suffers from tuberculosis and HIV while the third, and the only female, died in January during childbirth.

Number Eleven

Another sister, Oriede, was always at war with an old woman in her dreams. They would fight till daybreak and the only moment of respite was when she was awake. By the time we met, she had been deported three times from England. She spoke fluent and perfect Queen's English but she could neither read nor write any language, not even Yoruba.

The truth is this. When God passes the judgement of death on witchcraft, it goes on to affect all the children born into that line. This explains mysterious illnesses, dry favours, failure at the edge of break through, academic frustrations and witchcraft magnets. It goes on to cause acidic hardship and wild Pentecostalism.

I once ran into a pastor who got so angry because he was sold a counterfeit material. As he was cursing the man, he was speaking in tongue, yet he would still go on to prophesy in the name of the Lord.

I ran into four beautiful sisters at our church in Atlanta, US. They approached me after the service and said they needed my attention. Their problem? They had no husband. They probably had been married off to the same spirit husband.

Some spirit husbands are so strange and bold that, after committing immorality with their partners, they put money under their pillows; and if any man dares to propose to the lady, he would receive the beating of his life. The same is the case, if a man has spirit wives.

SOLUTION

It would be unfortunate if you just read this book, enjoy the story and laugh it off.

What is your foundation? What does your name mean? Why not get out of this situation by giving your life to Christ and thereafter pray violent prayers?

After your repentance, renounce foundational witchcraft, wage warfare against this power so that the blood will not cry against you again and, thereafter, pray for spiritual repair of those things already damaged and then finally pray a barricading prayer that will prevent them from returning.

As you pray it's better to lose your voice and have a sure foundation and a better future, than to be gentlemanly.

PRAYER POINTS

1. All my blessings in the custody of witchcraft, be removed by fire, in the name of Jesus.

2. Witchcraft calendar for my life, die, in the name of Jesus.
3. Every witchcraft covenant against my (career, academics, marriage, promotion, etc) die, in the name of Jesus.
4. Every altar of failure sponsored by witchcraft power, I tear you down, in the name of Jesus.
5. Power of God, push my stubborn Pharaoh into the Red Sea, in the name of Jesus.
6. Every fundamental arrow of witchcraft, backfire, in the name of Jesus.
7. Voice of my glory, be louder, be clearer than the voice of witchcraft, in the name of Jesus
8. Every virtue of my life buried by foundational witchcraft, come alive, in the name of Jesus
9. Foundational witchcraft of my father's house, die, in the name of Jesus.
10. Foundational witchcraft of my mother's house, die, in the name of Jesus.
11. Every voice of witchcraft from the grave be silenced, in the name of Jesus

12. Arrows of witchcraft from the moon and sun, backfire. in the name of Jesus
13. Foundational witchcraft, die. in the name of Jesus.

Chapter 5

THE MYSTERY OF THE HOLE IN THE WALL

MYSTERIES OF THIS WORLD

There are lots of mysteries in the world. If you don't understand the mystery, you may not understand certain occurrences.

We live in an age of warfare. The devil has unleashed violent terror upon the world. Therefore, there are certain things that are happening today, which never happened some fifty years ago. The only means of survival in this life is to be taught of the Lord and be given the keys of winning the end time battle.

We are considering a topic that may not sound very familiar. When we talk about 'the hole in the wall', we are referring to a very mysterious subject. Just as the devil has his own destructive strategies, God has designed certain strategies for saving and delivering His children.

You may ask, what is the hole in the wall all about? You shall soon discover the full import of this all-important subject. Unknown to many people there can be a hole in the wall. This is by no means physical; it is completely spiritual.

At this point you need to ask God to open your spiritual sight to see the hole in the wall. I want you to take this prayer point right now.

O heavens, today, arrest ever arrester, in the name of Jesus.

For proper understanding of this topic, we shall read a fairly long passage.

Ezekiel 8:7-18:

*And he brought me to the door of the court; and when I looked, behold
a hole in the wall. 8Then said he unto me, Son of man, dig now in the wall:
and when I had digged in the wall, behold a door. 9And he said unto me,
Go in, and behold the wicked abominations that they do here. 10So I went
in and saw; and behold every form of creeping things, and abominable
beasts, and all the idols of the house of Israel, pourtrayed upon the wall
round about. 11And there stood before them seventy men of the ancients
of the house of Israel, and in the midst of them stood Jaazaniah the son
of Shaphan, with every man his censer in his hand; and a thick cloud of
incense went up. 12Then said he unto me, Son of man, hast thou seen what
the ancients of the house of Israel do in the dark, every man in the
chambers of his imagery? for they say, The LORD seeth us not; the LORD
hath forsaken the earth. 13He said also unto me, Turn thee yet again, and
thou shalt see greater abominations that they do. 14Then he brought me
to the door of the gate of the LORD's house which was toward the north;
and, behold, there sat women weeping for Tammuz. 15Then said he unto
me, Hast thou seen this, O son of man? turn thee yet again, and thou
shalt see greater abominations than these. 16And he brought me into the
inner court of the LORD's house, and, behold, at the door of the temple
of the LORD, between the porch and the altar, were about five and
twenty men, with their backs toward the temple of the LORD, and their
faces toward the east; and they worshipped the sun toward the east.*

17Then he said unto me, Hast thou seen *this,* O son of man? Is it a light thing to the house of Judah that they commit the abominations which they commit here? for they have filled the land with violence, and have returned to provoke me to anger: and, lo, they put the branch to their nose.
18Therefore will I also deal in fury: mine eye shall not spare, neither will I have pity: and though they cry in mine ears with a loud voice, *yet* will I not hear them.

HOLE IN THE WALL

This is clearly an uncommon passage. If you are a good reader of the Bible, you would have discovered that the book of Ezekiel is a unique book. If you go through the first seven chapters of the book of Ezekiel you would have discovered that Prophet Ezekiel spent much time bringing the word of God to the people, but they did not listen. He prophesied to them but the word spoken did them no good. Against this backdrop, the Lord began to reveal to Ezekiel what had gone wrong with the children of Israel.

Interestingly, this is exactly what is going on in the church of God today. The situations within several Pentecostal churches bear resemblance to what happened in the day of Ezekiel.

Ezekiel the prophet had been in the spirit for a very long time. The fact that the spirit of God led him made him to discover that there was a hole in the wall. Someone who lives in the flesh cannot see into the spiritual realm. The barrier of the flesh will stand between the hole in the wall and the carnal believer.

God took Ezekiel to the door of the court. He was surprised to discover that there was a hole in the wall. Prompted by the spirit of God, he dug a hole in the wall and discovered that there was a door there. This door led him to see the wicked abominations of the children of Israel. What he saw was simply frightening.

Do you know that this kind of thing is still going on today? The fact that many people do not see this thing does not remove the fact that they are happening.

Very deep spiritual mysteries take place in the spiritual realm. It takes someone whose spiritual sight has been sharpened by the Lord to discover or detect these strange happenings. What we see on the surface may resemble beauty or excellence, but behind this facade are things that leave much to be desired. We shall soon discover the reality of these occurrences in today's world.

I want you to take this prayer point at this point.

Anything in my life that will bring Your anger upon my life, O Lord, deliver me from it, in the name of Jesus.

If you take a look at the ninth chapter of the book of Ezekiel you will discover that the Lord swung into action because of the children of Israel's refusal to obey the word of God.

Ezekiel 9:1-7

He cried also in mine ears with a loud voice, saying, Cause them that have charge over the city to draw near, even every man *with* his destroying weapon in his hand. 2 And, behold, six men came from the way of the higher gate, which lieth toward the north, and every man a slaughter weapon in his hand; and one man among them *was* clothed with linen, with a writer's inkhorn by his side: and they went in, and stood beside the brasen altar. 3 And the glory of the God of Israel was gone up from the cherub, whereupon he was, to the threshold of the house. And he called to the man clothed with linen, which *had* the writer's inkhorn by his side; 4 And the LORD said unto him, Go through the midst of the city, through the midst of Jerusalem, and set a mark upon the foreheads of the men that sigh and that cry for all the abominations that be done in the midst thereof. 5 And to the others he said in mine hearing, Go ye after him through the city, and smite: let not your eye spare, neither have ye pity: 6 Slay utterly old *and* young, both maids, and little children, and women: but come not near any man upon whom *is* the mark; and begin at my sanctuary. Then they began at the ancient men which *were* before the house. 7 And he said unto them, Defile the house, and fill the courts with the slain: go ye forth. And they went forth, and slew in the city.

Do you know what happened in this passage? God invited

the territorial angels and assigned them the duty of sending judgment upon the ungodly. One of these angels came with a pen. This particular angel was instructed to place a particular mark upon the forehead of all those who were displeased with what was going on.

In other words, those who wanted to live the holy life as well as those who did not want to offend God were supposed to be identified and marked. God decided to begin a fearful thing with the ancient men. That flagged off a divine visitation that was fearful and frightening to the core. Do you know what happened next?

Ezekiel 9:8-11

And it came to pass, while they were slaying them, and I was left, that
I fell upon my face, and cried, and said, Ah Lord GOD! wilt thou destroy
all the residue of Israel in thy pouring out of thy fury upon Jerusalem?
9Then said he unto me, The iniquity of the house of Israel and Judah *is*
exceeding great, and the land is full of blood, and the city full of
perverseness: for they say, The LORD hath forsaken the earth, and the
LORD seeth not. 10And as for me also, mine eye shall not spare, neither
will I have pity, *but* I will recompense their way upon their head. 11And,
behold, the man clothed with linen, which *had* the inkhorn by his side,
reported the matter, saying, I have done as thou hast commanded me.

Ezekiel was obviously sad about the situation. He tried to appeal to God. But as far as God was concerned there was no going back. Before Ezekiel could end his plea, the executioner had concluded his assignment.

All these things started through a hole in the wall. The elders were doing something that was completely wrong. To make matters worse, they got involved with what can be described as international, national, communal, family and personal witchcraft.

Only a hole in the wall could have discovered their evil activities. You may ask, how were they detected? It was simply through the revelation power of the Holy Ghost. What we need today is this kind of power. We need to pray fervently in other to receive this kind of revelation gift. You need to cry unto the Lord saying, "I want to be able to see a hole in the wall." You must say this prayer hard and strong. Tell God to show you whatever is being done against your life. Perhaps, if you handle this kind of prayer point effectively you will be able to know where you are going.

I want you to learn certain important lessons from the life of a brother who experienced a touch of the Lord along this line. The brother was so disturbed by the situation that he kept on crying to the Lord, "O Lord, give me revelation. I want to know what is happening to me.

He kept on bombarding heaven until God gave him an answer. One glorious day, an angel appeared to him with this message. "I have been mandated by God to take you somewhere. As I do this, promise that you will be silent."

He promised to comply. The angel of the Lord took him somewhere close to a big rock. The angel smote the rock and a big door opened. The brother and the angel entered through the door and the door was closed. To the surprise of the brother, the angel was taking him to a witchcraft meeting. Surprisingly, the meeting was yet to get started. They kept a little distance from the witchcraft meeting, waiting for the members' arrival.

I want you to cast your mind back to the fact that when Ezekiel was watching what the ancients were doing he was invisible. If you must make progress, you need to pray that God should make you to see the hole in the wall. When you know what the enemy is doing in your life you will know how to destroy the works of the devil.

If you know when demons gather, you will know how to scatter them. It is tragic that many of us pray only after witchcraft meetings have been concluded. We lose sight of the fact that to allow them to conclude their meeting is completely unwise.

If you sleep all night and you decide to bind demonic activities when you wake up in the morning, you are simply undertaking an exercise in futility. We need to know what we are doing. We need to pray to God to show us the hole in the wall.

Let me get back to the brother's story. By the time members of the witchcraft group started arriving, the brother noted that the first person to arrive was his former girl friend. He tried to scream but the angel quickly ordered him to remain silent. More members began to arrive. To his surprise, he discovered that all the ladies whom he had proposed to get married to came for the meeting. More members trooped into the evil meeting. At last, they waited for the overall leader to arrive. As soon as the leader emerged, all the members of the witchcraft group stood at attention. To his amazement he discovered that the leader of the group happened to be his mother.

He found it difficult to believe what he was seeing. The meeting went on and the agenda centred on steps to take in order to pull down Christian believers. A lot of strategies were discussed. At the end they came up with a strange decision.

"We shall destroy and dismantle the prayer lives of these people who call themselves Christians." They evolved a strategy to rob Christians of their power.

Why don't you take this prayer point?

Every witchcraft operation against my destiny, be exposed and disgraced. in the name of Jesus.

A lady once came to me and complained about her predicament. I encouraged her that God was going to bring a change into her situation. She believed the Lord. I gave her some prayer points urging her to pray fervently; She prayed with the totality of her strength.

All of a sudden, she screamed, "Doctor, come immediately. Some invisible hands are flogging me." She was rolling on the floor. Surprisingly, by the time we examined her back we discovered that there were marks. Everyone one was shocked. Nobody could see those who were beating her, but the physical marks were there all the same. This is the reality of spiritual warfare. How can we explain the fact that she had marks all over her body, without anyone around lazing her back with ugly stripes?

She prayed some prayers, which opened certain doors. The enemy got angry because the sister attempted to unravel the mystery behind her problems.

I want you to know that, a lot of mysterious things are going on around you. Without a hole in the wall you will not know anything about it. A lot of things are going wrong. You should be able to know what is really happening. Evil powers hold meetings every day. The devil has vowed that he is going to drag as many people as possible down to hell fire. He has vowed that he will not allow multitudes to fulfil their destiny. You need a hole in the wall. This is the most effective means of fighting spiritual warfare. You need to identify the forces that are confronting you.

A brother had an unusual experience sometimes ago. He had a dream, which bothered him. He saw some people frying what looked like delicacies on the fire. To his surprise, the angel of the Lord told him to peep into the pot. When he looked at the content of the pot he discovered that they were frying his placenta. The brother never understood the reason behind his rough experiences in life until he had this revelation.

The sight he saw made him to pray like a wounded lion.

He called the fire of God upon them, as he knew that his travails could be traced to what powers of darkness were doing in the secret. That was how he dislodged the agents of darkness that were harassing his life.

SEVEN ABOMINATIONS

Do you know that satanic agents who are carrying out evil things in the book of Ezekiel were doing seven specific things? This is made clearly visible in Ezekiel 8:10.

Here are the seven things.

Every form of creeping things.

These are satanic animals sent forth by the enemy to be programmed to the lives of men and women, to harass them in their dreams, thereby causing problems for them. These evil animals are dispatched by powers of darkness. Creeping things are demonic weapons.

Someone prayed the other time and a life lizard came out of her. Another person prayed and a long millipede came out of his nose. Many creeping things are programmed into the lives of people.

Beasts

The second group consists of abominable things; beasts. This kind of beast comes in form of serpents, leopards, Hyena, owls, vultures etc. The beasts represent particular spirits. Their main preoccupation is destruction. They work as agents in the hands of demonic powers.

Idols

The idol of the children of Israel was portrayed on the wall. Do you know that every idol has his own controlling demon? Again, every idol has an altar, a voice, a location, and his own power. According to Ezekiel's revelation, all the idols were displayed on the wall in order to enable them carry out evil activities.

Many of us are struggling with idols. Most of us come from idolatrous background. You may be a believer today but your ancestors were chronic idol worshippers. Many of us were given names which were attached to idols. These kinds of names had been written in the register of the devil. Although you may be living in an urban centre, your family members who live in the villages are still busy consulting with the devil.

Do you know that some idols are still been worshipped by

your parents on your behalf. This is an eye opener.

Wicked elders

There were ancient wicked elders. Seventy of such wicked elders were behind the problems of the children of Israel. Such powers are always busy monitoring the destruction of the lives of people. Wicked elders are scattered everywhere. They are busy programming destruction against God's people.

Burning of incense

Some of the satanic agents were busy burning incense. Thick evil incense surrounded the environment. That was how they carried out evil against the people.

Weeping for the queen of heaven

Some satanic agents were also busy weeping for the queen of heaven. Do you know that satanic agents can sit down for a long time and go into a funeral dirge upon the lives of someone who is still alive? It is an abomination.

Worshipping of the sun

Twenty-five men turned their backs from the house of God and faced the East worshipping the sun,. What were they doing? They were drawing powers from the heavenlies and baptizing the people with demons. This was a terrible problem.

Do you know that these seven wicked abominations are still going on today? The only thing is that the devil uses different methods to keep millions of people under perpetual ignorance. Unless God grants you a hole in the wall, you will not understand what is happening.

Many people live as if the devil has gone on holidays. They do not know that there are lots of problems going on in the world. Many people turn deaf ears to the preaching of sound doctrine. They try to protest saying that their Pastor is trying to place them inside a straight jacket. The day such people know that they can detect what the enemy is doing through the hole in the wall they will no longer handle the word of God with levity.

If God could grant you insight into what powers of what darkness are doing against your life, you will sit up. Do you know that the enemy is wickedly wicked? I wish there is another way of describing the evil that lurks within the heart of the devil.

Recently, I during my ministration in UK, a man was carried into the deliverance service. The sight was simply terrific. The man was so attacked by demonic powers to the extent that he began to undertake a project of self-destruction. With clenched fists he began to box himself. Without anybody attacking him he was raining heavy blows on himself.

When I questioned the wife, she told me that the man had been beating himself for six years. You would have thought that after a few blows, which the man inflicted upon himself, he would have rested for some time. The man never did. This is an example of wickedness of the enemy.

I want you to take this prayer point.

Every vulture in the spirit realm, hunting for my spiritual life, scatter, in the name of Jesus.

If the Lord should open your eyes one day, you will no longer joke with your spiritual life. If God should decide to show a little of what the enemy is doing you will always stand on your toes. Your prayer life will automatically change.

This reminds me of the story of a man of God who entered an aircraft. He observed that the fellow sitting next to him was busy praying aggressively. The man continued his prayers for thirty minutes. The man of God was both challenged and surprised. Out of excitement he asked about the church, which his seat-mate was attending. The man responded in a very strange manner. With a fierce countenance he charged at him: "I am not a Christian. Do you know what I was doing for the past 30 minutes? I was praying against Christians so that their marriages will fail."

The man of God was so surprised about the conduct of the strange prayer man, that made up his mind to pray until the plane landed. If you have not witnessed such an event, he would not have prayed.

Don't wait until you are shocked before you begin to pray. If you can pray fervently, God will show you the hole in the wall. When you behold the hole in the wall, you will discover that there is an array of wicked spirits who hate to see you progress in life. If the Lord has taught you how to pray fire prayers, you better be serious. If you do not prepare for the raining day, you may be confused when trouble comes. Do you know that your enemies are holding night meetings against your life? They do this constantly without any rest. These powers are working tirelessly to cause trouble for the people of God.

If you come across any believer who does not show any sign of being in touch with heaven such people deserve our pity and prayers. It shows that they have such a great problem. Such people do not know that the enemy of their souls is working with their fingers to the bone, in other to destroy them.

They are programming problems into the lives of those who are careless. They are also in charge of the duty of programming lukewarmness into the lives of those who are careless.

I have emphasised time and again that you are your own best prophet. Believers who roam from place in search of prophets are wasting their own efforts and time. Unfortunately, many of these people only go-to collect demons from the so-called churches or prayer houses. By the time the enemy has succeeded in dealing with them they run back to Mountain of Fire and Miracle Ministries. These people have turned us to fire brigade personnel. They refuse to follow the simple principles of holiness and spiritual warfare. They run helter skelter to where they burn their fingers through demonic consultations.

Many people are not willing to read the word of God, and

obey His commandments. They are busy looking for instant breakthroughs, which never come. They think that they can receive the blessing of God without repentance. They want to hold on to their pet sins and continue to pray for the blessing of God.

The secrets of many of them will soon come out in the months and years ahead. More secrets are going to come out at the end of the day. Many of us will come to terms with the fact that the greatest prophet we can ever have is yourself. If your spiritual torch is dead do not ever expect any prophet to come to your aid. Your greatest strategy is the 'do-it-yourself' method.

I want you to close your eyes and pray aggressively like this,

Any power, expanding my problem, die, in the name of Jesus.

If you are determined to fulfil your destiny, you must be sure that the kind of evil gathering which you have discovered in the book of Ezekiel may be programmed against you. You may not easily believe this, but one of these days, you will find out that God's word will ever remain true. God will grant you a vision of a hole in the wall. Reality will dawn on you. Then, you will become extremely careful with the way you handle your life.

Beloved, this is the wrong time to backslide. Do you know that if you backslide today the devil will make it impossible for you to trace your way back to God? The kind of stumbling blocks which he placed in the pathway of backsliders these days show that the devil is very wicked. But he can only succeed in destroying those who are careless.

I have said it, time and again, that I will never allow the devil to destroy me. The devil knows, for example, that the moment you fall into fornication or adultery you can be sure that sexual demons from the last seven partners of the person you get involved with will invade your life. This shows that the problems of that person will be combined with your own problem. You can imagine what will happen when you carry the problems of seven people.

Thus, anyone who goes into immorality with one demon will gather forty-nine wicked demons. The enemies know that such people are breaking the laws of God. They will move in swiftly with a fresh baptism of violent demons. When such people come for deliverance ministration, they would not tell us the whole truth.

It is easy to sin but the consequences can be suffered for years. The Bible is very clear it says, "Although hand is joined with hands a sinner cannot go unpunished." You will be more careful when you learn this spiritual truth.

CONSEQUENCES OF EVIL GATHERING

The moment you have the kind of evil congregation described in the book of Ezekiel congregating against your life you have a lot of work to do. You will begin to notice the following things:

☞ Backward progress

This is a serious problem. You may not make progress along the right direction. Instead of going forward you will begin to go back.

☞ Attack from star reducers

You may begin to experience the activities of wicked powers. For example, they may begin to suffer the attack of star reducers. Your star may be very bright but they may begin to darken it.

☞ Attack from swallowers of money

You may suffer the attack of powers that swallow money. You will only discover that the powers behind your finances are affecting you negatively.

☞ Attack from powers that arrest progress

You may also detect the activities of powers that arrest progress. Do you know that some wicked satanic agents are busy chanting demonic verses night and day in order to work against you? Some of these people's experience sleepless nights just because they want to pray wicked prayers against you.

☞ Meaningless dreams

You may also begin to have meaningless dreams. This is another satanic strategy

☞ Rain of affliction.

☞ Strange money may be found in your purse or possession.

☞ Amputated breakthroughs.

You may suffer problems that can be traced to

amputated breakthroughs.

These are the problems that the enemy has programmed against many people today.

The solution to all these problems resides in God granting you a hole in the wall. Once you are given this kind of spiritual revelation the devil will not be able to harass you.

KEYS TO CREATE A HOLE IN THE WALL

The question, which you are likely to ask at this point, "Is how, can I create a hole in the wall? How can I receive the kind of revelation that will forever change the pattern of my prayer?"

The answer has been provided in the Scriptures. Do you know that Ezekiel was not able to detect a hole in the wall until he had preached from chapters one to seven? By the time he got the eighth chapter he saw a glorious revelation. Behold there was a hole in the wall.

It is interesting to note that when God wanted to deal with people concerned he dealt with them summarily. There was no mercy. The only people who were spared were those with a mark on their forehead.

What then are the keys to getting a hole in the wall?

This key can be made available to those who are serious with God. The moment you begin to pray the prayer points listed at the end of this chapter you will begin to experience supernatural events.

For example, you may suddenly find yourself inside a witchcraft meeting, to your surprise you may discover that you are the subject of their discussion. You may be too shocked to pray at that moment, but you will have to pray all the same. The kind of revelation, which God is going to grant you, may shock you. You can only get this revelation if you make up your mind to be more serious with God.

☞ Ask the Lord to reveal your own veil to you.

Let Him show you what is blocking your vision.

☞ Ask the Lord to remove every cover of darkness.

Let Him deal with everything that is blocking your spiritual vision.

☞ Ask the Lord to clear away spiritual cataracts in your

eyes, so that you can see what you are supposed to see.

Let me close this chapter with a particular experience, which a sister had.

This sister noticed that each time she went to work and return home the temperature of every one of the her children was unusually high. She did not understand what was actually happening. One day she went to work as usual. The Holy Spirit gave her a strange message as soon as she arrived the bus stop, "Daughter, go back home".

Initially she found it difficult to understand the instruction given to her by the Holy Spirit. However, she managed to obey. By the time she arrived home she observed that her three children were screaming in a very strange manner. She peeped through the keyhole and experienced the greatest shock of her life. She saw the housemaid sitting at the centre of the living room and surrounded by her three children who were screaming.

But the sight was indeed sordid. The house girl was half human and half snake. Her head was the head of the house girl while the rest of the body was that of a serpent. The woman shouted, "Jesus."

Before she could know what was happening the house girl has transformed her self into a human being. The house girl quickly pretended as if nothing was happening. The woman spell bound. She could not utter a word. The woman could not conceal her shock. She said, "Young girl, so you are a serpent."

To the amazement of the Christian woman the house girl impudently replied, "Madam, with all the Bible you carry about and your commitment in the church you mean you never knew I was a serpent? Who killed your husband?"

The Christian woman could not believe her ears. Why don't you say this prayer point now?

Thou blindness of the spirit, clear away, in the name of Jesus.

You must deal with every form of spiritual blindness. Get ready now, for a prayer session that will turn your life around.

POWERS TO ATTACK

One thing is certain immediately you decide to fulfill

your destiny, be very sure that the whole of hell fire will rise up against you. Do you know that there are powers that do not want you to live a holy life? There are powers that have vowed to prevent you from getting to heaven. There are powers that would be happy to see you match blindly towards hell fire.

There are powers that hold vigils in order to prevent you from experiencing your breakthroughs. There are powers that specialise in giving church post to people in other to tie them down and prevent them from making heaven their focus.

Some power specialises in promoting Christians beyond their Christian experiences or level of spirituality. These powers are working night and day just to introduce spiritual demotion into the lives of men and women.

There are powers that have no other job but to steal, kill and destroy. There are powers that are angered by our kind of prayers. You must tackle these powers.

Now that you are being given the keys to experience a hole in the wall, you must scatter all kinds of demonic meetings that had been held against your spiritual and physical well-being and you will experience breakthroughs if you can pray at that moment. Now get ready to pray.

PRAYER POINTS

1. Every agreement, made by my ancestors with dark powers, die, in the name Jesus.
2. Thou wicked ancestral power, die in the name of Jesus.
3. Every water and animal powers in my family line, I destroyed your agreement, in the name of Jesus.
4. Every spiritual marriage, with water spirit, die, in the name of Jesus.
5. Every evil, spoken against my destiny before I was born, die, in the name of Jesus.
6. My enemy shall acknowledge the finger of God, in the name of Jesus.
7. I reject, every evil authority, in the name of Jesus.
8. Every satanic transfer of evil names, I destroy you, in the name of Jesus.
9. Every power, supervising evil family altars, die, in the name of Jesus.

Chapter 6

THE SECRET OF SEEING THE HOLE IN THE WALL

YOUR SPIRITUAL EYES MUST BE OPENED

You cannot appreciate the importance of divine revelation until God opens your eyes and makes you to see what is going on in the spiritual realm.

Let us take a second look at a mystery passage in the book of Ezekiel 8:7-18:

And he brought me to the door of the court; and when I looked, behold
a hole in the wall. [8]Then said he unto me, Son of man, dig now in the wall:
and when I had digged in the wall, behold a door. [9]And he said unto me,
Go in, and behold the wicked abominations that they do here. [10]So I went
in and saw; and behold every form of creeping things, and abominable
beasts, and all the idols of the house of Israel, pourtrayed upon the wall
round about. [11]And there stood before them seventy men of the ancients
of the house of Israel, and in the midst of them stood Jaazaniah the son
of Shaphan, with every man his censer in his hand; and a thick cloud of
incense went up. [12]Then said he unto me, Son of man, hast thou seen what
the ancients of the house of Israel do in the dark, every man in the
chambers of his imagery? for they say, The LORD seeth us not; the LORD
hath forsaken the earth. [13]He said also unto me, Turn thee yet again, *and*
thou shalt see greater abominations that they do. [14]Then he brought me
to the door of the gate of the LORD's house which *was* toward the north;
and, behold, there sat women weeping for Tammuz. [15]Then said he unto
me, Hast thou seen *this*, O son of man? turn thee yet again, *and* thou
shalt see greater abominations than these. [16]And he brought me into the
inner court of the LORD's house, and, behold, at the door of the temple
of the LORD, between the porch and the altar, *were* about five and
twenty men, with their backs toward the temple of the LORD, and their
faces toward the east; and they worshipped the sun toward the east.
[17]Then he said unto me, Hast thou seen *this*, O son of man? Is it a light
thing to the house of Judah that they commit the abominations which

they commit here? for they have filled the land with violence, and have returned to provoke me to anger: and, lo, they put the branch to their nose. [18]Therefore will I also deal in fury: mine eye shall not spare, neither will I have pity: and though they cry in mine ears with a loud voice, *yet* will I not hear them.

The lost blessings of spiritual benefits

Several years ago we used to run the school of prophets. In those days, we used to gather participants together for a three-day dry fast; for complete three days no food, no water. Those who participated did so with joy and excitement. In those days people valued spiritual things more than material concerns.

It is surprising, these days, that the Power Must Change Hands fasting and prayer programmes which lasts for only one full day and a few hours has given a lot of people problems. In those days, people were very happy to fast. But today's generation has lost sight of the power of spiritual benefit. This is the tragedy of this generation.

Ninety five percent of the letters that are sent to us these days border on material benefits. It seems that our generation has decided to place more value on material benefits above spiritual things. We used to experience the divine presence of God during our spiritual programmes in those days.

To understand what is really happening you must come to terms with the fact that the present situation can be traced to the problem of misplaced priorities. Our sense of value has changed.

I can recall a particular incident, which happened during one of such spiritually anointed programmes. A sister was praying somewhere within the congregation. As she continued her prayer, she beheld a strange sight. There was a giant man in dazzling white apparel standing at the rear end of the church building. The eyes of the angelic personality were red. The sister became frightened. For a very long time the sister kept on looking at the angelic personality. For quite a long time she did not know what to do. For the first time in her spiritual life the Lord opened her eyes to behold supernatural sights. It was an unforgettable experience. The Lord had started to open her eyes to see beyond the physical realm.

As soon as the service was over, she decided to pay a visit to her prayer partner and share her new experience. By the time she got there she saw a fellow eating rice and beef. But instead of the normal food the fellow was eating she discovered that the rice was covered with blood. When she was invited to join in the eating, she simply declined, she had seen what others couldn't see. She left the place for her own house. On the way she began to feel sorry for herself. She wondered what had been happening to her. Under normal circumstances she would have eaten the rice.

Beloved, if you are not careful and your eyes are not open you may eat human blood. You may not know that you are eating demonic food. That is why the Bible says, "My people perish for lack of knowledge." I want you to stop reading for a moment. Place your right hand on your head and take this prayer point, with the vigour of a wounded lion.

O God, arise and open my spiritual eyes, in the name of Jesus.

The first thing that must happen to you is that the Lord must open your spiritual eyes.

What is the second step which you must take in order to be divinely empowered to see a hole in the wall?

YOU MUST DESTROY THE OLD MAN.

The old man is your greatest enemy, an enemy of God, it hates holiness, an enemy of heaven, is the satanic friend hibernating in your life.

As soon as man fell in the garden of Eden, and lost all the beautiful things that God planned for him, the state of the heart of man has been referred to in the Scriptures as the old man.

The old man is a terrible entity. It is the carnal nature, which lives inside us. It is the remains of sin, which has vowed not to leave us alone. It can also be referred to as inbred sin.

As long as you continue to allow the old man to have his way in your life, your spiritual eyes can never see anything. This would be so simply because it is impossible to be in the camp of the enemy and be allowed to spy what is going on.

The old man makes you a person who cannot rise to the level of sonship. Wherever the old man is thriving, the Spirit of God will only be an observer. Many of us had been crying to God saying: "O God, use me. I want to hear Your voice and see heavenly vision", but cannot receive the answer of heaven to their requests. Until such people deal with the old man, God can never give them a vision. God is telling you, as long as you remain close to the old man, you cannot see the glory of God.

This reminds me of the vision of one of our most respected Pentecostal fathers. He prayed fervently saying: "O Lord, there are many babies in this church. What shall we do? O Lord, intervene. Make them to grow. Give them power. Let them receive revelation knowledge."

The man of God was so burdened that he cried unto God for seven days and seven nights. At the end of the programme, God gave him a revelation. He saw a caterer who has lots of palatable dishes to give out. The food had a good aroma and was steaming hot. On the other side he saw a long queue of his own church members, waiting to be served. Each of them was carrying his plate. He noticed something that is unusual. The caterer was weeping bitterly. Those who were on the queue waiting for the food were also weeping. Some of them were even wailing saying, "Please, give us food. We are very hungry."

The caterer was also crying saying, "I am ready to give you food, but your plates are dirty, and contaminated. If you can check your plates carefully, you will discover that there are faeces in it."

This is exactly what is wrong with many of us today. You are crying for power of divine revelation, but you are not ready to keep your vessel clean. The ways of God are very simple. Whenever you meet the condition, He gives you what you are desired. The Bible makes it very clear. It says, "The Lord does nothing without revealing it to His servants, the prophets."

Do you know that as you are reading this book there are people who know what will happen in Nigeria for the next ten years? There are people who know the details of what God is going to do in the church in the next five years. These people are not special human beings. Nothing stops you from becoming one of them. What you need to do is to kill the old man.

Many Christians are having problems. It is because the old man is alive and well in their lives. If you ever come across Christians, who are telling lies, you can be sure that the old man is still very strong in their lives. If you ever come across Christians, who fight publicly it shows that the old man is still kicking in them.

Pride, seed of old man

One other way of detecting the presence of old man is by spotting evidences of pride in the lives of the so-called Christians.

Pride is the old man's most powerful weapon and it is evil. It threw down angels from heavens. It was pride that turned good angels to devils. God never created a devil. He created Lucifer. The Greek meaning of the word pride is very revealing. It is likened to something swelling like a balloon. This means you are trying to appear above your real level. It is an index of self-exaltation.

Pride is extremely bad. Several other sins are attached to it. Many people would never steal if they were never propelled by pride. Most people who steal are not ready to live a humble life. They want to live big. Hence, they decide to join armed robbery gang.

Pride gives you a feeling of being superior to others. This means that you have decided to over-price yourself. You want to take on a stature that is larger than life. You may begin to feel that you are above others, simply because you think you are bigger or richer than they are or because of your possessions, talent, education, or contacts in the society. The simple truth is that you are prideful instead of being humble. The old man is alive and well in you. Such a person cannot see the hole in the wall.

The life of people with pride will be filled with

contentions, strife, division, wrangling, evil speaking, discord and the like.

If we all gather and our prime objective is the glory of God, nobody will be proud. The moment you feel that you are better than every other person the old man is in place.

If you listen to some people talk about their academic degrees or certificates, you might become sick. Some people feel that to let others know that they are specially qualified they must frame their certificate and hang it on their necks. They want everybody to know that they have a Master's or Doctorate degree. Some people go about telling those people who care to listen to them that their parents are the first lawyers or engineers to qualify in the country. All these attitudes are sponsored by pride.

Some people exhibit pride in the church by saying, "I can't join that group. The members do not fit into my class. What would I come here to do if not that there was no better place to go?" This is pride.

Some people refuse to participate in group projects saying: "Why did they elect me as the chairman? They do not seem to respect my academic qualification." It is pride.

"Why can't they show some respect to me? They should recognise that I have a Master's degree. Why should I be grouped with all these uneducated folks? Pride.

Why did they not put my name on top of the list? Pride.

Some ministers even go to the extent of saying, "Why are people saying faint 'amen' to 'my prayers'? Other people would say, "I cannot use any vehicle unless it is air-conditioned, I know my class. Nobody can ever make me to join the bandwagon."

Pride has assumed new dimensions. Do you know that it is possible to be proud of things like immorality, spiritual gifts, abilities, talents, dressings etc?

We have been telling our sisters these days that our Sunday worship services are not meant for any form of fashion parade or carnal showmanship. Thank God, many of them are learning how to drop their bogus outfits. They now know that the house of God is the house of prayer.

Friend, nobody wants to know how costly your clothes are. Dressing the old man is nothing but sheer waste of time and resources. To dress the old man is to behave like a blind bat.

Some people are busy manifesting the character of the old man. They say things like, I cannot worship in a place where I am not noticed. I go first-class everywhere. Whenever I entered my former church everybody stood at attention. Why am I like a common fellow here? Why am I not given recognition?

Some people are simply incorrigible. If you ever correct them, they react sharply. As long as you exhibit this kind of trait you will never see anything. You will continue to have fellowship with demons, bad dreams and demonic attacks. Evil night caterers will feed you every day. Demonic barbers will continue to find marks on your body. Of course, demonic agents will visit you regularly since the old man is alive in your life.

Anger, seed of the old man

For so many other people the old man manifests its ugly presence through anger. When you offend some people, they will continue to boil internally. The life of such people can be likened to a volcano that is about to erupt.

Many homes have been destroyed through anger. A lot couples have divorced themselves through anger.

You must kill the old man!

Recently someone asked me questions: "G. O. can I take part in the Holy Communion? I have not paid the whole of my tithes?"

The answer is very clear. Do not take part in the Holy Communion if you are a thief. To rob God in tithes and offering is to be a thief of the highest kind. How can you steal from God and take part in His flesh and His blood?

There is a church in this country where many died like houseflies by partaking in the Holy Communion wrongly. They took the Holy Communion while they held on to their sins. There was no iota of repentance in them. God visited them in judgement.

At the same time, if you avoid taking the holy communion, it shows that you are not yet on your way to heaven. You need a change of life. You can only begin to see hole in the wall when you have completely repented of your sins.

EVERY HIDDEN FOUNDATION MUST BE SHAKEN

Ask God to shake every hidden foundation in your life. All evil hidden foundation in your life must be uprooted. This is very important.

At this point, I want you to close your eyes and lay your right hand on your navel. Get ready to take this prayer point.

Foundation of darkness in my destiny, die, in the name of Jesus.

Recently, I visited the MFM branch in London. A counselee came for prayers and deliverance. She looked at me frankly and said, "Someone told me about you and I decided to come to see you. I know that you are a prophet. I think you can be of help to me."

I told her to go on, assuring her that I would do whatever I could to help her. She opened her bag and brought out an exercise book. She told me that she had five children. The name of the first child was written on the first page, the second on the second page, the third on the third page and so on. The woman had three boys and two girls.

I was surprised when I discovered that the woman wanted me to help her choose one out of the ten names which appeared eligible to marry her first daughter. That was how she wrote names of prospective partners for her children. I asked to know how she got all the names. She simply told me that she compiled them by writing down the names of all those who came to visit her children. She handed the exercise book over to me, asking me to make the right choice, as a prophet. However, she honestly told me that she had made similar requests in other places. A lot of parents are still doing the same thing today.

Let me share a story with you.

A particular woman suffered terribly because she had a strongman attached to her destiny. When she married the first husband, she woke up around 2:00 a.m. on the night of her wedding only to discover that the man was placing his two legs on the wall. She woke him up but the man kept on lying down like a log of wood. She shook him violently. It took the man five minutes before he opened his eyes.

She received the greatest shock of her life when the man said, "Never you make this mistake again for the rest of your life. Whenever you see me in that position, be sure that I have undertaken a spiritual journey. If you ever touch me, you are in trouble. However, I am going to discipline your father and your mother for what you have just done."

By the time the sister woke up the next day she was told

that her father and mother had died. She was so frightened that she packed out her load and ran out from the man's house.

Five years later, she got married to another man. Just as soon as she had gotten married, the new husband woke up at exactly 2:00 a.m., dragged her to the door at the boy's quarters where he told her, "Let me warn you. Don't ever open this door. If you ever try it, you will die."

She was so confused that she did know what to do. One day, she came under so much pressure that she decided to open the door. On opening it, she saw a lifeless old woman that was as dry as stockfish. She discovered that the woman was carrying a calabash. To her surprise, wads of currency littered the ground. She almost fainted. That was how she packed out and backed out of the second marriage.

She kept on marrying the wrong people. I want you to close your eyes and take this prayer point.

Every error sponsored by being bewitched, clear away, by the blood of Jesus.

Wipe out all satanic demands and agreements

made with your ancestors, by the blood of Jesus.

You may not know the kind of agreement or covenant which your forefathers or ancestors have made. For example, they might have covenanted all your family members to a lifetime of untimely death, failure at the edge of miracles, and poverty. They might have also made a covenant to the effect that everybody who eats *ókro* in this family will never succeed. They might have agreed that none of their family members would stop worshipping idol. A great curse would have been placed on those who violate such deep agreements.

Unknown to you, such agreements may be in place and if you fail to cancel them and you violate them ignorantly, your efforts will not yield any positive result. The devil will torment you and God will never show you a secret. You must cancel all negative agreements.

Silence every evil voice that is speaking against you

Unknown to many people, all kinds of voices are speaking against them. The voices speaking against you may be the voices of the babies which you have aborted. It may the voice of the lady who decided to take her life or who ran mad or suffered mental depression after she was jilted that is crying against you.

The voice crying against you may be the voice of the altar of your ancestors. Gideon suffered because a voice was crying against him. He was supposed to be a mighty man of valour yet he lived like a slave. He lived far away from where he was supposed to be. There was something in his father's compound speaking against him.

Deal with all voices that are speaking against you.

Destroy the time clock of the devil

Do you know that the devil has his own clock with which he controls the destiny of men and women? He operates many lives without a clock. You must stop the clock from controlling your destiny.

Destroy every evil blood covenant

Cut such covenants off completely. As long as any form of blood covenant continues to control your life your destiny may never be fulfilled. Your spiritual eye may never remain open unless you cut off every evil blood covenant.

Cut off every evil attachment with heavenly beings.

Take prayers of slaughter against demonic beings.

If you can carry out all these steps, you will be amazed at the kind of revelation which God will grant you. God will show deep things about what is going on in secret places concerning your life.

I shared a very important experience during one of our Power Must Change Hands programmes. There was this very wealthy sister whose life was upside down. She ran from place to place in search of help. To make matter worse, one of her friends offered to take her to a very powerful fetish priest or 'herbalist' as they are called in Nigerian English.

When the sister got to the house of the herbalist, she was surprised to discover that the man was a cripple and was an illiterate. The highly-educated and wealthy sister was shocked when the fetish priest told her that the only way of receiving solution to her problem was to allow him to sleep with her. She turned back and decided to look for solution in another place.

Her friend persuaded her to consider what the fetish priest was saying. She told her that was exactly what she did during her own time of crisis. "Why don't you do it and get over your problem?" she said.

She decided to close her eyes and allow the fetish priest to commit immorality with her. She took off her clothes and waited for the fetish priest. All of a sudden she heard the voice of the herbalist from underneath the bed saying, "Carry me."

The lady got sick of the whole situation, put on her clothes and ran out of the herbalist's house. She decided to perish if she would, instead of dancing to the tune of the fetish priest. That was how somebody directed her to me.

As soon as she came, she was given some prayer programmes. She began to see an egg suspended from the ceiling of the room. That was how God granted her the opportunity of seeing a hole in the wall.

She went to her mother, armed with some questions. "Is there anything in my history that has something to do with suspended eggs?"

The mother answered, "Yes, there is this particular issue. In those days, when I was pregnant, I was always suffering miscarriages. I consulted a fetish priest who carried out a ritual which has something to do with a suspended egg. That was how I gave birth to you." The sister discovered, for the first time in her life, that her life had been suspended like an egg.

A lot of things are happening in this world. The kind of prayer at the end of this chapter goes beyond what should be handled carelessly. The kinds of prayer you will pray in order to be granted access into divine secrets are not ordinary ones. You must pray with every strength within you. You must pray fervently to be given an insight into the spiritual realm. At that point nothing will ever scare you. You will be confident, no matter what evil powers are trying to say.

Are you not tired of living like an unbeliever? Why should you fail to know what is going on in your life? Now is the time to cry unto God to convert your dreams to visions. Ask God to take you beyond the level of dreams to the realm of revelations. Pray until God begins to open your eyes to the secrets of your enemies.

Chapter 7

THE STRANGERS SHALL WITHER

Many Christians today are suffering seriously and they do not know the sources. Affliction plagues them day and night and they begin to wonder what is happening. The enemy has so concealed his machinations that the Bible calls them strangers,

Psalm 18:44-46:

As soon as they hear of me, they shall obey me: the strangers shall submit themselves unto me. [45]The strangers shall fade away, and be afraid out of their close places. [46]The LORD liveth; and blessed *be* my rock; and let the God of my salvation be exalted.

These same verses can be read as follow:

"Stranger shall fail, the aliens shall wither." It can also be read as: "The stranger shall lose their hearts and shall come trembling out of their closed places. Another way of reading it is, they will come quickly out of their strange places, and they shall come trembling out of their strong hold. One thing that is striking in all these variation is that is "the stranger shall wither."

WHAT OR WHO IS A STRANGER?

A stranger is simply a thing or an object that is residing in or occupying the wrong place. A person becomes a stranger when he leaves his home and country for another that is not familiar. An object becomes a stranger when it leaves its normal abode; for example a pair of scissors in the stomach, chain in the heart and so on. When these happen, they are strangers.

These strangers usually have their abode where the Bible calls closed places or strongholds. These strangers usually have their strong holds deeply hidden. They are always very difficult to locate, and to destroy, but when dangerous and violent prayers are prayed, and their strongholds are challenged, then that which Bible says shall occur; the stranger shall fade away and be afraid out of their closed places.

LIFE EXPERIENCES

It happened once, that we prayed for a woman who had been pregnant for 18 months and when she went into labour, a very strange thing happened. She delivered a black nylon bag! The question now is this, how did this nylon bag enter into her body?

At Mountain of Fire and Miracles Ministries in Port

Harcourt, live animals came out of people. A live rat came out a person and it was caught, kept in a bottle and the picture was taken.

Some people have been delivered of live animals after undergoing deliverance at the Mountain of fire and Miracle Ministries Prayer City. When you see live snakes and rats, coming out of people that are alive, you begin to wonder; How did they get there? There is no way a person harbouring live animals in him can live a meaningful life.

There are cases in which whole living beings have walked out of people all because they dared to challenge the strangers and their strongholds with hot prayers.

There was a brother who was wallowing in abject poverty. Not satisfied with his situation, he prayed some terrible hot prayers and in broad day light, not in a dream or vision, he saw an old man dressed in rags looking like a beggar walked out of him. The old man moved forward, turned and waved at the brother and the brother waved back at him; that was the end of his poverty, lack and want.

Maybe, you are reading this book and you are wallowing in poverty or you are not satisfied with your condition take this prayer and the Lord will surprise you.

By the power of the Holy Ghost, I move from where I am to where I am supposed to be, in the name of Jesus.

There was a time when a paralysed man was brought to one of our meetings, and as we prayed, this man actually felt something coming out of his head and he grabbed it.

The more the prayers, the longer the object and by the time we finished, the object measured the width of a ruler and as tall as the man himself. It was brought out and he received instant healing. Who on earth could have convinced him that a ruler had been programmed into his life? Or who can convince a man that another living being resides in him?

There was another case of a woman, who, after a prayer meeting, felt like using the toilet and came back with two living mud fishes that came out of her! This was at the MFM church in Jos, northern Nigeria. Now, how did these fishes get into her?

I have seen so many situations where strange things came out of people and I have heard of so many cases in which crawling animals came out of people.

There are many people in these situations but who do not

know how to break free or set themselves lose. The Bible says in the book of Matthew 11:12 that

Matthew 11:12

And from the days of John the Baptist until now the kingdom of heaven suffereth violence, and the violent take it by force.

The Bible passages above makes mention of violence and the violent. How else can one describe the presence of animals, nylon bags, rulers and other strange objects in the body, except wicked violence?

These spirits are very clever and they usually conceal their strongholds deep in their host. They are continually corrupting, perverting and destroying every segment of life and human beings. They are carrying out their mission of killing, stealing and destruction almost unhindered. This free access, which they enjoy, is because of ignorance. Man is ignorant and this allows them to operate unmolested and because there is no resistance they initiate internal decay that leads to external destruction.

This is the devil's strategy.

THE OPERATIONS / ACTIVITIES OF STRANGERS

Some people do not seem to know that life is a battle and that there are powers that govern the universe where we live in.

Many a time, we experience internal struggles or confusion. This implies that there is a stranger there in. When these strangers are not challenged, they exert an influence over one's life. One may think all is well and that he is doing fine but that 'fine' may be the lowest level of the things God has in stock for you.

The time has come to look within us and not outside for the enemies. Your wife is not the enemy, neither is he any of your children. Rather, deep inside of you lies the great enemy hidden. These hidden enemies are the ones responsible for the dreams, nightmares and they enjoy immunity because you are binding what is on the outside rather than what is on the inside.

They are also responsible for the death of good things in the lives of people. They engineer failure at the edge of breakthroughs. Mysterious financial failures and many other afflictiors are part of their activities.

These hidden killers also intensify the warfare of the enemy on the people. Their activities on the inside allow their cohorts on the outside to boast and one begins to wonder why. They are inside you, working hard to ensure that you do not progress.

You may be tempted to say you have no stronghold in you, but if you would pray sincerely and challenge them violently, they will come trembling out of their closed places and you will see the difference in your life.

It saddens me to know that, many people are operating below God's level for their lives. Many people have potentials but these have been buried, all because there is a stranger hiding in a closed place.

Life does not permit a vacuum; nature does not leave gaps and God does not create gaps. At anytime, somebody or something has to be in charge. Every empty space must be filled. Your life has to be controlled either by God or the devil, the choice is yours.

There is this testimony of a man of God, who went into seven days dry fast with a deliverance candidate. On the seventh day, as the man of God prepared to break his fast, the Lord made him to see the inside of the candidate.

Right there was a throne and a king sat on it; the Lord said to him; for seven days you have fasted and prayed with this man but you have only sent the messengers and house boys packing, the king is still there. Now do you want to break your fast or continue?

Many people go for deliverance and at the slightest appearance of victory or breakthrough, they quit yet the king remains on the throne. You need to be extremely violent.

SORTS OF STRANGERS

Hidden strangers in closed places are basically of two sorts.

Evil spirits.
Evil deposits.

Some people are always eating or being fed in the dreams, these constitute evil deposits. Though they may have stopped eating in the dream but the fact is that these things are still there, deeply hidden and they must be destroyed.

Some have been having spirit husbands and wives visiting

and depositing things in them, they may have stopped but their deposits need to be destroyed.

Strangers in the body include programmed hidden sicknesses, spiritual padlocks, evil marks and identifications. All these things have their set time, they wait and watch for the weak hour and then they strike violently. But if you would get violent with holy anger, their works would certainly be destroyed.

There was the case of a girl, that saw the mark '666' on her body. She got to school and showed her teacher. Thinking it was all a joke, she instructed her to wash it off but when the girl explained that she had been washing for hours and upon a closer look, the mark was found to be on the inside and not outside, that was the end of school for that day. Similarly some people would wake up only to find scratches all over their body, it is an evil mark.

Animals, as we have already seen, can be programmed into the life of a person and as the person moves or progresses, the animal moves and progresses too.

Employing demonic house-helps also bring about strongholds and strangers. These demonic beings that do the cooking will initiate almost all, if not all the household.

The food they cook does not join the digestive system but stays aside to do its evil assignment. They are evil deposit and must be destroyed totally.

Strangers can also be described as dematerialized objects. This usually confounds people, making them to think it impossible. How does one explain a continuos pounding in the head as though a mortar where were being used? How does one explain the presence of a nylon bag in the womb? These things are first de-materialized before they are programmed.

Strangers in the body also refer to wicked human spirits that can get out of their original owners and begin to influence the lives of others.

Strangers also refer to evil blood and growths. You hear of sudden and mysterious cases of anaemia, leukemia, fibroid, cancer, ulcer, kidney, stones and so on, they are all strangers that will flee their strongholds if only we would pray.

Failure or refusal to address these strangers is a direct invitation to evil visitors that divert good things away and cause bondage. The woman was bent for 18 years. For 18 years she was in bondage, and had good things diverted from her. But when she met with Jesus, He ordered her to be loosed. Strange as this prayer may be, but it worked. Jesus could see the rope binding her and He ordered it lose.

Refusal to deal with strangers and stronghold, causes people to commit unpardonable mistakes. It creates internal sicknesses, provides ladder for satanic attacks facilitates sudden death and destruction.

They need to be dealt with. As they act as internal smugglers, they pass virtues to the enemies, kill, steal, destroy and cause confusion. These are terrible cowardly powers that will surely run out, if only you would pray with all sincerity and from the bottom of your heart.

Beloved, it is not enough to just read and say the prayers, you need to digest every word in this book and pray, violently, all the prayer points. It is time you moved ahead in life.

STEPS TO FREEDOM

How can you experience freedom from these kinds of problems?

To be free would require a great amount of violence on your part. You need to get violent in your spirit with your situation and pray violent prayers.

To be free, you need to surrender your life to Jesus. You must repent from and forsake all forms of sins.

You must also decide in your heart to hate the strangers with perfect hatred and that you want to be free.

You must also curse them and speak destruction unto them as you pray to root them out.

Finally, you pray barricading prayers that will prevent them from returning to your life. It is recorded that when an unclean spirit has left a man, it does not go far, rather it stays close looking at the place where he had been sent out and when he sees that the place is clean and garnished, he will now say, "I will return to my house," and if the place is unoccupied, he invites seven more wicked spirits and the end is therefore worse than the beginning.

It is very sad, to know that two spirits can control a person's life. The example of Saul readily comes to mind. He was prophesying, yet he was tearing his clothes. This was possible because Saul was an unstable character. He was violent, self-willed, envious and temperamental. All these combined to finish him off.

Finally, two things determine the rapidity of your deliverance.

Level of secret sin. What is that thing that you engage in, in the secret? The more they are, the slower your release.

Secondly, your background. If your background is that of pronounced idol worship or occult activities, you need to be extra violent and aggressive while praying the following prayer points.

If only you would pray, all those things, which have been pronounced dead, would come alive. All the cages used to hold you back would be broken.

PRAYER POINTS

1. Holy Ghost fire and thunder, pursue my pursuers, in the name of Jesus.
2. Strangers of darkness in my life, wither, in the name of Jesus.

3. Every owner of evil load in my body, I command you to carry your load, in the name of Jesus
4. Every arrow of the night, come out by fire, in the name of Jesus.
5. Every herbal power, working against my destiny, what are you waiting for,? die, in the name of Jesus.
6. Strangers of infirmity, depart by fire, in the name of Jesus.
7. I fire back, every arrow of untimely death, in the name of Jesus.
8. Every arrow fired into my life as a baby, die, in the name of Jesus.
9. Every habitation of witchcraft in my family line, die, in the name of Jesus.
10. Oh God that answers by fire, answer me by fire, in the name of Jesus.
11. Every waster of my prosperity, be dismantled, in the name of Jesus.
12. Every power, working against my comfort, die, in the name of Jesus.
13. Every dream of poverty, I dash you into pieces, in the

name of Jesus.

14. Every anti-prosperity altar in my compound, die, in the name of Jesus.
15. Every dry bone in my finances, come alive, in the name of Jesus.
16. Oh heavens, open on my prosperity, in the name of Jesus.
17. I fire back every arrow of spiritual rags, in the name of Jesus.

The power of the father's house of Moses prevented him from entering the promised land. The power of the father's house of Gideon caged his destiny. The power of the father's house of David landed him in adultery and murder. The power of the father's house of Solomon entrapped him in the prison of strange women.

Unless a man cuts off the evil flow from the powers of his father's house, he will not fulfill his destiny. In order to assist the generation of Gehazi, one must revisit the curse issued upon him by Elisha.

This is one book that will cause ripples in the kingdom of darkness.

Many prisoners will receive their freedom, buried destinies will be exhumed and turbulent cases will be divinely fixed up, as the powers of the father's house are kept under divine check.

About BCCM, MFM Ministries and the Author

Dr. Daniel Kolawole Olukoya, is the General Overseer of the Battle Cry Christian Ministries, and Mountain of Fire and Miracles Ministries (MFM). The Mountain of Fire and Miracles Ministries' Headquarters in Lagos, Nigeria is the largest single Christian congregation in Africa with an attendance of over 120,000 in any single meeting.

MFM, is a full gospel ministry, devoted to the revival of Apostolic signs, Holy Ghost fireworks, miracles and the unlimited demonstration of the power of God, to deliver to the uttermost. Absolute holiness within and without, as the greatest spiritual insecticide, and a pre-requisite for heaven, is openly taught. MFM is a do-it yourself gospel ministry, where your hands, are trained to wage war, and your fingers to do battle.

Dr. Olukoya, holds a first class honours degree in Microbiology, from the University of Lagos, Nigeria and a PhD in Molecular Genetics from the University of Reading, United Kingdom. As a researcher, he has over seventy scientific publications to his credit.

Anointed by God, Dr. D.K Olukoya is a prophet, evangelist, teacher and preacher of the Word. His life and that of his wife, Shade and their son, Elijah Toluwani are living proofs that all power belong to God.

The Battle Cry Christian Ministries is devoted to:

(a) teaching and disseminating information on Christian spiritual warfare,
(b) making available, life-changing Christian articles and books, at affordable prices and
(c) preparing an army of aggressive prayer warriors and intercessors in this end-time.

Published by:
The Battle Cry Christian Ministries

ISBN 978-35755-6-2